HOMESCHOOLING GIFTED KIDS

Homeschooling Gifted Kids:
A Practical Guide to Educate and Motivate Advanced Learners
Copyright © 2018
Our Journey Westward, LLC

No part of this book may be reproduced, translated, stored in a retrieval system, or transmitted, in any form or by any means, electronic, mechanical, photocopying, microfilming, recording, or otherwise, without written permission from the publisher.

At the time of this book's publication, all facts and figures cited are the most current available; all telephone numbers, addresses, and website URLs are accurate and active; all publications, organizations, websites, and other resources exist as described in this book; and all have been verified. The author and Our Journey Westward make no warranty or guarantee concerning the information and materials given out by organizations or content found at websites, and we are not responsible for any changes that occur after this book's publication. If you find an error or believe that a resource listed here is not as described, please contact Our Journey Westward.

Our Journey Westward, LLC
https://ourjourneywestward.com
naturexplorers@gmail.com

ISBNs: 978-1-7324003-0-6 (pbck), 978-1-7324003-1-3, (epub)

Publishing and Design Services: MartinPublishingServices.com

HOMESCHOOLING GIFTED KIDS

A Practical Guide to EDUCATE & MOTIVATE Advanced Learners

Cindy West, M.A.Ed.

"I'm in the trenches homeschooling gifted kiddos, and while it's a lot of fun… it can be a challenge. Cindy's book was such a blessing! As I read through it, I found myself nodding, dog-earing (gasp!) pages to come back to or share with my husband, and feeling like someone was finally able to relate to my day-to-day homeschool."

—Colleen Kessler, M.A.Ed.
Award Winning Educator, Gifted Specialist, Podcaster,
and Founder of RaisingLifelongLearners.com

"Cindy is intensely practical, and although she discusses educational philosophies, most of the book delves into specifically how to teach children. I love how she sprinkled specific examples from her own children throughout the book. She includes book lists, activity ideas, and lots of hints. Homeschooling Gifted Kids covers all the academic areas, telling how to prod a student who does not excel in that area as well as how to challenge a student who does."

—Jimmie Quick, M.S.
Owner of iHomeschoolNetwork.com
and Co-Creator of Homeschool.Marketing

"Parents of gifted kids are often intimidated about how to meet the needs of their students. Other books I've read on this topic have left me scratching my head – confused about where to begin. Cindy does a wonderful job of making teaching advanced students practical, simple, and fun. The chapters on 'Teaching All Learners' and 'Individualizing Instruction' are alone worth the price of the book."

—Marcy Crabtree
Gifted and Special Needs Blogger at BenandMe.com

"Many parents of gifted and advanced children decide to homeschool so they can provide a rich learning environment only to find they are overwhelmed or do not know how to challenge such students adequately. Cindy West, a veteran homeschooler and publisher of NaturExplorers, shows how homeschooling children who are gifted can be a joy and doable for any parent. She rests your mind and equips you through helping you understand learning styles and strategies to use in your homeschool."

—Richelle McFarlin
Co-Owner of TalkingMom2Mom.com

"Cindy is a veteran homeschooler with gifted children; she knows what she's talking about. She includes practical ideas, websites, and resources, not just pie-in-the-sky theories. She also addresses practical ideas for those who struggle in certain areas, including how to find curriculum that will challenge your advanced learners. She helps parents think through the best course of action for each student. This is not just a one-size-fits-all solution manual. Cindy even incorporates practical ideas on how to find creative outlets for talented kids and how to find true intellectual peers."

—Bethany LaShell
Veteran Homeschooler and High School English Teacher

"The standard perception of a gifted child is that of a trailblazing high achiever. In truth, that standard perception is wrong. West maintains an incredible grasp of the unique nature of the gifted child, excels in communicating that knowledge, and offers a practical, approachable toolbox for home educating parents. *Homeschooling Gifted Kids: A Practical Guide to Educate and Motivate Your Advanced Learners* is a must-read for any family educating gifted children at home."

—Ginny Kochis, M.A.
Gifted and Twice-Exceptional Advocate at NotSoFormulaic.com

This book was eye-opening. I learned the definition of giftedness. The different types and areas of giftedness. Plus, *Homeschooling Gifted Kids: A Practical Guide to Educate and Motivate Your Advanced Learners* armed me with the tools and ideas needed to meet the needs of my gifted learners. Maybe you know that your student is gifted in a particular area but aren't exactly sure how to foster that giftedness. Cindy's book will encourage and inspire you as well as offer the practical strategy to put in place for learning!"

—Tricia Hodges
Owner of ChalkPastel.com
and Author of *Help! I'm Homeschooling!*

"I found *Homeschooling Gifted Kids* when I was preparing a presentation on the topic. I was most impressed by its thorough review of the best resources to use with advanced learners. While it is a book focused on gifted kids, I recommend it to any homeschooling parent wanting to educate with excellence."

—Melanie Wilson, Ph.D.
Psychologist, Author of Grammar Galaxy, Podcaster, and
Founder of Psychowith6.com

"Cindy has done a terrific job of lining up resources for homeschooling parents to equip them for working effectively with their gifted kids. The book piqued my curiosity because meeting a gifted learner where he was is the reason we began homeschooling in the first place. It's the reason we began and it's the reason we continue to press on in this endeavor."

—Heather Woodie, M.S.
Creator of Homeschooling High School by Design
and Homeschooling for College by Design
and Owner of BlogSheWrote.org

Contents

Introduction 1

Why Homeschool Gifted Children? 3

An Overview Of Homeschooling 13

Choosing Curriculum 39

Teaching All Learners 57

Technology and the Gifted Homeschooler 95

Individualizing Instruction 109

Organizing Your Homeschool Day and Record Keeping 125

What About Socialization? 137

Thinking About College 149

Frequently Asked Questions 157

Resources 171

References 197

About the Author 201

Introduction

Homeschooling can seem like a daunting task, while homeschooling a gifted or advanced child can seem downright unmanageable. I'm here to help. By the end of this book you will have the information and tools you need to homeschool your gifted child with confidence and joy!

I will hold your hand as you begin to think about things like choosing curriculum, planning schedules, and finding homeschool groups. I will help you discover your child's learning styles and most appropriate learning environments. I've included tons of practical ideas, both secular and religious, for meeting your child's exceptional or twice-exceptional needs in just about every subject area under the sun.

But, don't think this book is only appropriate for the new homeschooler. Any parent of a gifted, advanced, or even twice-exceptional student who needs to reevaluate or revamp his or her homeschool will find fresh ideas and encouragement to pursue a purposeful and exciting path. You'll learn new ideas for everything from record keeping, to project-based learning, to integrating technology into your homeschool in creative ways. Heck, I've even included a chapter on college planning!

Why am I qualified to write such a book for you? Well, I've been homeschooling unofficially for 21 years (since my oldest was born), and officially for 18 years (the time when I had to start submitting records to my local board of education). All three of my children have been homeschooled from the very beginning, all are gifted in various ways, and all are doing exceptionally well in their studies. I also happen to have a master's degree in education and speak regularly to parents across the country about homeschooling, meeting children's specific needs, and teaching in creative ways.

My hope is that you will find this book incredibly practical, helpful, and easy to read. My prayer is that you and your child (or children) will enjoy an abundantly fruitful life while homeschooling.

chapter 1

Why Homeschool Gifted Children?

My Story

I was a gifted child. Not a genius by any means, but a little girl who had great academic and leadership potential. However, it wasn't cool to be smart. Once I realized, by upper elementary school, that heading to gifted and talented classes made me stand out from the crowd in less than desirable ways, I quickly learned to hide my abilities.

Even if I hadn't, by middle school, the only special classes available to me were a logic elective in seventh grade and an accelerated algebra course in eighth grade. I still maintained my position in these accelerated classes and continued to make good grades, but no one prodded me, or any of the other gifted students, to reach for the stars. And most of us were very glad of that because reaching for the stars meant almost certain insult from our peers.

At least in elementary school we had a gifted teacher who encouraged us to excel, and we had each other to be "different" with. Without that sort of encouragement and camaraderie in middle school, by high school I was really no different on the outside than the cool group that I so desperately wanted to be part of. So, like many gifted children, especially girls, I "lost" my giftedness in order to fit in. I still took upper level classes, made good grades, and got into my chosen college without a hitch, but I didn't reach the potential that was in me – and I knew it.

As I began my career teaching elementary children, I was keenly aware of the peer pressures placed on children as young as second grade to fit in. Each year I taught in the public school classroom, there were very clear lines drawn between those who were smart, those who were gifted in other ways that made them different, and those who were what most would call "normal" (or typical) students. The third group always determined themselves to be the cool ones, while those who were gifted were placed outside of their circle. Very seldom did a child cross over the lines to be part of more than one group. As the school year went on and children were pulled from my classroom for special classes, the lines became even more pronounced.

As much as I tried to erase those lines as the teacher, encourager of gifts and talents, and encourager of acceptance for everyone, there was little I could do. It was very eye opening for me to watch my own story unfold as 7- and 8-year-old children would "lose" their giftedness in order to fit in.

I'm now the mom of three children who are all gifted in one way or another. I didn't set out to homeschool from the moment my first child was born because, for some reason, I believed in the school system that had failed me so. I believed in the school system in which I was teaching, even though it was crumbling right before my eyes. Young children were facing peer pressure, they were being introduced to adult issues around every corner, teachers had their hands full with discipline issues, teaching was being dumbed down so everyone could learn, courses were taught that didn't line up with my beliefs, and the list goes on.

Once I was faced with the reality of sending my first, precious, innocent child into that atmosphere, I couldn't do it. So, in short, I didn't begin homeschooling with the idea that I needed to meet the needs of my gifted children. In fact, quite honestly, it's been through homeschooling that I've come to see their giftedness!

> **homeschool hint**
>
> Although you may know your child is gifted or advanced in one or more areas already, keep your eyes open for new interests and gifts that will reveal themselves as you spend more time learning alongside your child.

What is a Gifted Child?

Before we jump right into the topic of homeschooling gifted children, I'd like to define the term gifted. As you may know, giftedness comes in many forms, making it difficult to narrow the term into one comprehensive definition. However, a very simplified definition is "having great ability or talent." Tables 1 and 2 give you more detailed definitions for various types of giftedness.

With each type of giftedness, there are very different methods of schooling to best meet the child's particular needs. There are so many, many examples of this, but I'll provide just a few simple examples to give you an idea of what I mean. (We'll definitely talk more about specifically meeting needs throughout the book.) For example:

- A child with a high IQ in math will need math curriculum that challenges him appropriately. He may or may not need above-average-curriculum for his other subjects.
- A child who is an exceptionally talented dancer will need time and opportunities to hone her dancing skills, while still making sure she is on track academically.
- A child with potential to achieve will probably need to work with his teacher when making curriculum choices so they both agree on motivating, challenging, and appropriate assignments.

Table 1. Giftedness Relating to Academic Achievement

High IQ	Children who score above 115-120 on intelligence tests are considered to have a high or gifted IQ. A score of 100 is considered the average IQ. The higher or lower the score from 100, the more need there is for educational modifications to meet the child's needs. Sometimes children have high IQs in some subjects, but not in others.
High Achievement	These children love to learn, have a great memory and do well on tests, projects and other assignments. You can often find high achievers scoring in the 95th percentile or higher on achievement tests. They also tend to have a large vocabulary, ask lots of questions, and get excited about learning.
Potential to Achieve	Children who have the ability to do well, but are unmotivated, uninterested, or not being challenged may not score well on tests or complete assignments efficiently. It's a little harder to bring out the potential, but it can be done.

Note. From ERIC Clearinghouse on Handicapped and Gifted Children (1990); National Association for Gifted Children (n.d.)

Table 2. Giftedness Relating to Exceptional Talent

Visual/ Performing Arts	These children have an extreme interest and/or talent in art, music, dance or drama. You will find they express themselves best through their particular mode, and often need very little instruction as compared to most children to be very good at what they do.
Creative Thinking	This talent could certainly fit in the academic achievement chart (Table 1) because of the ability this child has to solve problems. However, it encompasses children who are comedic, inventors, rule benders, and great arguers, too.
Leadership	Children gifted with leadership ability are able to take on a lot of responsibility, organize, make decisions, and often speak well. They expect a lot from themselves and those around them.

Note. From ERIC Clearinghouse on Handicapped and Gifted Children (1990); National Association for Gifted Children (n.d.)

- A creative child who is constantly pushing boundaries might need to help her teacher write a behavioral contract to keep her on track with assignments and responsibilities.

As you can see, there is no cookie cutter approach to teaching gifted children! In reality, there's no cookie cutter approach to teaching any child. Homeschoolers have an awesome opportunity to personalize instruction to meet the specific learning needs of each child.

Why Homeschool a Gifted Child?

As we've just seen, each child – gifted or not – has his own needs. The homeschool parent not only instinctively knows those needs most of the time, but also can offer the flexibility and resources necessary to meet them much better than a classroom teacher who has a large number of students. The classroom teacher has an overwhelming responsibility to attempt to meet the needs of each child, but often that just isn't possible. She will do her best to group children according to ability level, offer some reasonable "extras" for the students who finish ahead of everyone else, try to use gifted and special education teachers to offer a little help, and so forth. But in the end, there is no way to help every single child excel to her specific ability. Trust me when I say I'm not putting down classroom teachers; many of them are very good at what they do! However, having been in their shoes (and having been a very good teacher in most people's eyes), I know for a fact that it's just not possible to be everything for every child.

So, in my mind, the biggest advantage to homeschooling a gifted child is that you get to meet his needs perfectly. Of course, there are several other advantages to homeschooling as you can see in Table 3.

Because I'm a very visual and concrete learner, I like to use charts and examples to give you better pictures of how homeschooling principles translate to real life. In this example, I'll use a scenario from my own home to show

Table 3. Advantages to Homeschooling Gifted Children	
Curriculum to Suit Ability	The homeschool parent gets to choose which leveled materials her child needs. If the child can work on math at the 10th grade level, but needs spelling on the 5th grade level, that's what the parent teaches.
Curriculum to Suit Interests	If a child is a history buff, the homeschool parent has some leeway to organize the material so that it includes more than the average amount of history. If that same child is creatively gifted, the parent could choose to assign creative projects about history to further meet his interests.
Assignments to Suit Learning Styles	If a child's learning style leans heavily on music, for instance, the parent can easily bring music into any lesson to enhance the learning.
Flexibility in Scheduling	School doesn't have to take place between the hours of 8am-3pm. If a child learns best in the afternoon, he can have school in the afternoon. If he wants to be part of a robotics club on Mondays, he can do the rest of his schoolwork on other days.
Time for Extras	Think for a moment about all things you've wished your child could take part in – the community orchestra, the travelling ball team, a community college course. These are much more manageable with a flexible homeschool schedule.
Time for Character Training	Like it or not, many gifted kids struggle in one or more character areas, like thinking before they speak, having low self-esteem, not being very organized, being too organized, and so on. The list could go on and on, and doesn't just include gifted kids! Homeschooling allows parents the opportunities to really work on some of the problem areas with their kids because they're home together more.
Time for Socialization	The biggest misnomer about homeschooling is that children don't get enough socialization. My calendar is forever full of social engagements! Also, because kids can find others on their ability level or with a similar interest area more easily, homeschool socialization rarely leads to feelings of not fitting in, which is a major issue for many gifted kids.

you the advantages we've enjoyed in homeschooling one of my children in particular.

My daughter has always been an avid reader. Her journey with reading started at the age of 4, and I'll estimate that she's soaked up nearly 1,000 books in the years since. She also has a passion for animals. I don't doubt that she would have done well in a regular school setting; however, all of the mechanics of school annoyed her. Besides math, she really didn't need the repetitive lessons and practice that most classrooms offer. She diligently completed hands-on projects, but rushed to get through them in order to spend more time reading. She read everything from historical fiction, to field guides, to books (and books and books) about animals.

At first, I was determined that she would be allowed to read, but "get everything else done", too. It didn't strike me until much later that she was naturally picking up some of the "everything else" simply through reading. In other words, she could describe an era of history accurately after having read three or four books on the subject, both historical fiction and nonfiction. She had picked up on most spelling rules and grammar usages simply from seeing them over and over again in her reading.

Once I began letting go of how I was "supposed" to teach certain subjects, and let her do it in her own way, she began to excel even more – and it took a lot of the pressure off me. Of course, reading isn't the only thing she did as schoolwork, but it became her main mode of gathering information.

homeschool hint

Always be willing to think outside the box when considering how a child is supposed to learn and what materials should be used for various subjects.

In some subjects then, such as history, she was accelerated. We worked together to design assignments that would motivate and challenge her, while at the same time allowing her freedom and flexibility to cover the material at her own pace. In other subjects, like math, she was right on target for her age and needed the daily lessons and practice. Because of this, she didn't have as much independence in deciding when and how to complete her math work. Did she like this? No, but she understood that I offered her as much independence as possible, at the same time requiring certain things out of necessity.

Allowing an amount of freedom to learn things that motivate our children has been one of the greatest rewards in homeschooling thus far. You see, my daughter's love for animals is not my own. If I had pushed curriculum to only meet my agenda, I would never have known the passion she has for animals. If I had pushed my own agenda every hour of the day, she wouldn't have had the time to develop her talents with animals. If I had allowed her no freedom to choose what she reads, she would never have read the hundreds of informational books about animals. But, because I took the time to notice my daughter's passion and encourage it, she knew as much about animals in her early high school years as some veterinary students in college!

homeschool hint

Capitalize on your child's interests whenever possible!

Can you see how this short example has included many of the sections from Table 3? My daughter was given curriculum to suit her needs and interests, I tried to meet her learning styles when possible, and I allowed her flexibility in learning and time to pursue her passion areas. In turn, she blessed me with motivation and excellence in most of her endeavors.

Are There Disadvantages to Homeschooling?

As much as I advocate homeschooling for most people, there are some disadvantages that I encourage every homeschooler to consider before taking the plunge (see Table 4). Some of these are especially pronounced when considering homeschooling gifted students.

Don't let the list scare you! Most of the considerations can be overcome if you're really willing to make homeschooling work. Becoming a more scheduled and organized person might be a new habit for *you* to work on as you begin teaching your child, for example. Or, you might decide to shop local curriculum sales and used curriculum sites online to find materials for less money. As John Burroughs said, "For anything worth having one must pay the price; and the price is always work, patience, love, self-sacrifice – no paper currency, no promises to pay, but the gold of real service." ("John Burroughs Quote," n.d.). Homeschooling isn't an exception.

	Table 4. Homeschooling Considerations
Time	It takes time to homeschool. Someone has to be the teacher. Even if you choose to hire a tutor or enroll your child in an online school, someone needs to be the child's caretaker. I've seen some families homeschool successfully while both parents work, but it takes organized effort.
Organization	The parent has to be organized enough to plan what curriculum her child will use and how the lessons will be completed. (It's okay if her child is part of the planning process.) If she isn't organized with the school work, chances are, her child won't take it upon himself to complete it.
Assignments to Suit Learning Styles	If a child's learning style leans heavily on music, for instance, the parent may need to bring music into a lesson to enhance the learning.
Discipline	I'm talking about two types of discipline here. The parent needs to be disciplined enough himself to stick with whatever homeschooling plan is designed. I've seen way too many homeschools fail simply because the parent couldn't get himself together to have lessons ready to go daily. The other type of discipline means just what you're thinking. The parent needs to know how to motivate his child to behave and obey. There are many ways to go about this, but the main point is that the parent has to make sure schoolwork gets done.
Patience	Some gifted kids tend to push limits. They creatively step over boundaries, get frustrated easily, want to challenge you or their siblings over every little thing, and so on. Parenting in general requires patience, but a homeschooling parent will be with her child a lot, so she needs an extra dose of patience.
Willingness	The parent has to want to homeschool. If she doesn't want to do it, the road is going to be much longer and harder. A positive attitude makes all the difference! The child doesn't necessarily have to desire to homeschool because the parents are the main decision makers. Most kids who've been pulled out of classrooms love homeschooling after a period of adjustment. Most kids who've never been in the classroom don't balk too much.
Money	Although some parents will feel comfortable designing their own curriculum very inexpensively, many will need to purchase at least some things. Costs vary greatly. Also consider the costs of classes, lessons, and special equipment to supplement your child's interests.

Chapter 2

An Overview Of Homeschooling

What is Homeschooling?

Before we get any further into the book, I suppose it might be important to define homeschooling. Just what is it, and is there only one way to do it? Homeschooling takes place when a parent or tutor teaches a child, usually at home, rather than the child going to a public or private school. That's the broad definition. There are actually many ways to accomplish homeschooling. I've outlined the main points of most homeschooling methods below.

Traditional Approach

This is the homeschooling method that looks most similar to the environment in a classroom setting. The parent usually buys student and teacher manuals for all subject areas and expects her child to complete a number of lessons per day. She will likely give her child tests provided with the curriculum and keep detailed grading records. She typically follows a daily and yearly schedule that coincides with the local school system.

Advantages to the Traditional Approach:

- ✓ Several companies offer curriculum-in-a-box which will provide you with an entire year's worth of lessons in every subject, plus teacher's guides.
- ✓ Because the schedule and lessons are most similar to a school setting, a child usually transitions very well from one to the other.
- ✓ The parent has a good grasp of how her child is doing in each subject and can tally grades easily.
- ✓ The boxed curricula are planned so that very few academic gaps are experienced.

Disadvantages to the Traditional Approach:

- ✗ Gifted children rarely fit into one grade level, so purchasing a set level will likely not fit the child in all subjects.
- ✗ Not all gifted children appreciate textbook/workbook style learning. Those who need to learn creatively or immerse themselves into interest-based studies will likely become frustrated with the necessity of keeping up with all of the daily assignments.
- ✗ Curriculum-in-a-box can be very expensive.
- ✗ If you are homeschooling more than one child, it's difficult to combine the children for certain subjects because rarely do two levels study the same topics.

AN OVERVIEW OF HOMESCHOOLING

homeschool toolbox

Some popular providers of traditional lessons include:

- Abeka – abeka.com
- Accelerated Christian Education – aceministries.com
- Alpha Omega – aophomeschooling.com
- Bob Jones University – bjupress.com
- Calvert School – homeschool.calvertschool.com
- Core Curriculum – core-curriculum.com
- K-12 – k12.com
- Moving Beyond the Page – movingbeyondthepage.com
- Oak Meadow – oakmeadow.com
- Rod and Staff – rodandstaffbooks.com

Unit Study Method

The unit study method often integrates all or most subjects into one theme, while immersing the student into one topic. Unit studies are often hands-on, activity-based, and literature rich and allow for flexibility in both scheduling and direction of study. Some people choose to complete unit studies based on history and science topics, while adding separate math and phonics curricula.

Advantages of the Unit Study Method

- ✓ Because of the flexibility of unit studies, gifted children can engross themselves into a theme of interest as long as they desire. When a certain aspect of the study sparks curiosity, they can go down a "rabbit trail" to learn more. For these reasons, unit studies can be very appealing to the engaged, gifted homeschooler who loves to learn.
- ✓ Without the time constraints of a traditional approach, a more natural flow to learning occurs.
- ✓ Unit studies are very easy to do with multiple ages at once. Everyone focuses on certain key information, while being allowed to pursue

trails, projects, literature, and so forth that appeal to their own levels and desires.
- ✓ It's fairly easy to tie together all subjects so that connections are made in learning.
- ✓ Things like hands-on activities, field trips, and other experiential learning naturally flow from unit studies.
- ✓ Prepared unit studies can be very inexpensive.
- ✓ Creating your own unit studies is not difficult.

Disadvantages of the Unit Study Method

- ✗ Because of the flexibility, it can be hard to keep distractible children on task or children who immerse themselves in study from going overboard.
- ✗ The teacher has to be good at preplanning, following through with the plans, and gathering a few materials.
- ✗ The teacher has to make sure all subjects are being covered at some point, especially math and various language arts.
- ✗ Because the children will be engaged in books, projects, experiments, recipes, and other learning experiences, it could mean some untidiness in the house.

Some popular providers of unit studies include:

- A Journey Through Learning – ajourneythroughlearning.net
- Beautiful Feet Books – bfbooks.com
- Five in a Row – fiveinarow.com
- Hands of a Child – handsofachild.com
- Heart of Wisdom – heartofwisdom.com
- KONOS – konos.com
- Moving Beyond the Page – movingbeyondthepage.com
- NaturExplorers – ourjourneywestward.com
- Sonlight – sonlight.com
- Tapestry of Grace – tapestryofgrace.com

Free unit studies can be found for almost any subject you or your child would like to ponder. Simply type "free unit study (insert topic)" into your Internet search engine and it should bring up several choices.

Classical Education

Classical education is a method of learning dating from the ancient eras of Greece and Rome. Its main essence is that children should be taught in certain ways depending on their cognitive development, resulting in the grammar, logic, and rhetoric stages of learning. During the grammar stage (typically early and middle elementary age), children are taught concretely and gather the basics of things like math, grammar, and foreign language. During the logic stage (typically late elementary and middle school), children are taught to think logically, analytically, and investigatively. And during the rhetoric stage (typically high school), children are expected to express themselves verbally and in written language. Most classical education experts suggest either two 6-year cycles or three 4-year cycles of repeating history and science topics. The study of Greek or Latin, philosophy, the arts, and classic literature are familiar characteristics of classical education, too (Bauer & Wise, 2009, Classical Homeschooling, n.d.).

Advantages of Classical Education

- ✓ It can be a very rigorous educational program and quite challenging for gifted learners who need more.
- ✓ By default, it provides children with the tools to learn and think for themselves.
- ✓ After reading a book or two about classical education, the parent can design his own curriculum using materials that will best meet the needs of his child, while still fitting into the classical framework.
- ✓ There is some flexibility to allow for independent study choices by the child. For instance, she will be able to choose what and how many books to read about a certain era of history. Also, the doors are open for adding extra or more challenging work, or, conversely, stepping the rigorous material down.

Disadvantages of Classical Education

- ✗ A true classical education can be overwhelming to both the child and parent academically. A lot is expected in order to complete every facet of this method. However, it's fairly easy to tweak things to make them work for your family.
- ✗ Although it can be done and takes some effort, it's hard to teach multiple ages the same material.
- ✗ A huge emphasis is placed on history and classical literature. If the parent isn't careful, it's easy to fall short on the sciences.
- ✗ Depending on the curriculum choices, the parent will probably need to be good at preplanning.

Two popular how-to books for homeschooling classically are *The Well-Trained Mind: A Guide to Classical Education at Home* (4th edition) by Susan Wise

Bauer and Jennie Wise, and *Teaching the Trivium: Christian Homeschooling in a Classical Style* by Harvey and Laurie Bluedorn.

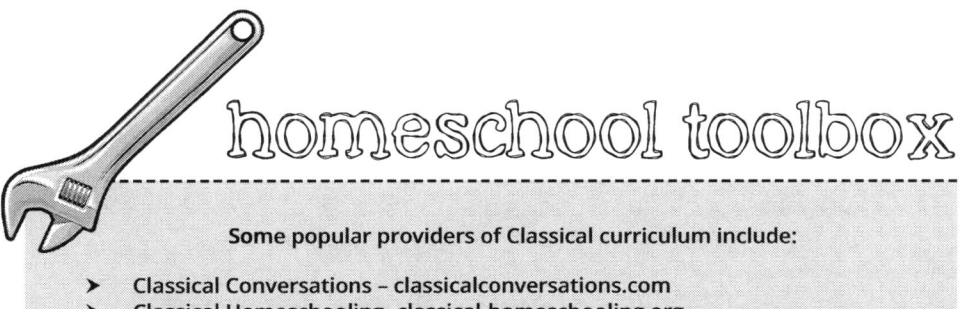

Some popular providers of Classical curriculum include:
- Classical Conversations – classicalconversations.com
- Classical Homeschooling – classical-homeschooling.org
- Covenant Home – covenanthome.com
- Easy Classical – easyclassical.com
- Memoria Press – memoriapress.com
- Tapestry of Grace – tapestryofgrace.com
- Veritas Press – veritaspress.com

Charlotte Mason Style

Charlotte Mason was a 19th century British educator who believed education was an atmosphere, a discipline, and a life. She believed in teaching children in ways that encouraged curiosity and enthusiasm, while at the same time expecting excellence in many areas – even more than most curricula expect. Besides the typical academic subjects, a Charlotte Mason education also focuses on art, music, poetry, "living" literature, nature study, handicrafts, and life skills through lessons that are short and to the point. This style even encourages such specifics as the importance of outdoor play and training good habits.

Advantages of a Charlotte Mason Style Education

✓ The format of short lessons that get right to the point are very good for children who don't like to waste time, as well as children who struggle with attention issues.

- ✓ The style of teaching lends itself to a very loving, exciting, and joyful atmosphere.
- ✓ Children are encouraged to be curious and make connections, which can benefit many gifted learners.
- ✓ "Living" literature, otherwise described as very well written books, makes learning meaningful and interesting.
- ✓ The basic style can be intertwined with other styles (e.g., classical) quite easily.
- ✓ For many of the aspects (e.g., nature study, art) multiple ages can be taught at the same time.
- ✓ Parents have freedom to make particular curriculum choices that best meet their child's needs.

Disadvantages of a Charlotte Mason Style Education

- ✗ This style allows parents to pick and choose curriculum, which can be overwhelming for some. However, more companies are beginning to offer curriculum sets and/or suggestions for a Charlotte Mason style homeschool.
- ✗ The teaching parent is typically very involved in the daily lessons.

homeschool hint

This is the basic style I use, while incorporating some bits and pieces of classical education and unit studies. It allows me the freedom to use strictly what my children need when they need it, while offering us a plethora of extras that help my children to become well-rounded.

A few popular how-to books for a Charlotte Mason education include *For the Children's Sake: Foundations of Education for Home and School* by Susan Schaeffer Macaulay, *A Charlotte Mason Companion: Personal Reflections on the Gentle Art of Learning* by Karen Andreola, *A Charlotte Mason Education: A Home Schooling How-To Manual* by Catherine Levison, and Charlotte Mason's own *Homeschooling Series*. The Original Homeschooling Series can be downloaded in its entirety for free at amblesideonline.org/CM/toc.html.

Some popular providers of Charlotte Mason style curriculum include:

- Ambleside Online – amblesideonline.org
- Homeschool Highlights – livingbookscurriculum.com
- Our Journey Westward – ourjourneywestward.com
- Queen Homeschool – queenhomeschool.com
- Simply Charlotte Mason – simplycharlottemason.com
- Winter Promise – winterpromise.com

Principle Approach

The Principle Approach is an educational method that uses the Bible as the cornerstone of every single subject, with an emphasis on God's providential hand throughout history. This style encourages children to take responsibility for their education, while the parent acts more like a mentor. Biblical thinking and reasoning are foundational objectives, as well as embracing the principles on which America was founded. It boasts excellence in the 4R's – research, reasoning, relating and recording (The Foundation for American Christian Education, n.d.; Homeschool.com, n.d.).

Advantages of the Principle Approach

- ✓ Children who prefer to take control of their own education might appreciate the independence offered.
- ✓ Christians will appreciate the Bible being held as the authority.

- ✓ Americans will appreciate the focus on our country's foundation and that they will be very versed in such things as the U. S. Constitution.
- ✓ Because parents are more hands-off in this approach than some homeschooling styles afford, they could find a little more free time throughout the day.

Disadvantages of the Principle Approach

- ✗ Because it's rooted deeply in the Bible, those wishing for a secular curriculum will likely not appreciate this approach.
- ✗ It involves lots of independent work on the part of the child. This could be too demanding for some children, especially those who have a hard time staying on task.
- ✗ Large amounts of reading, writing, and research are foundational in this style. Some will find that an advantage, while others will find that a disadvantage.

Two popular how-to books on this style are *A Guide to American Christian Education for the Home and School: The Principle Approach* by James B. Rose and *Teaching & Learning America's Christian History: The Principle Approach* by Rosalie Slater.

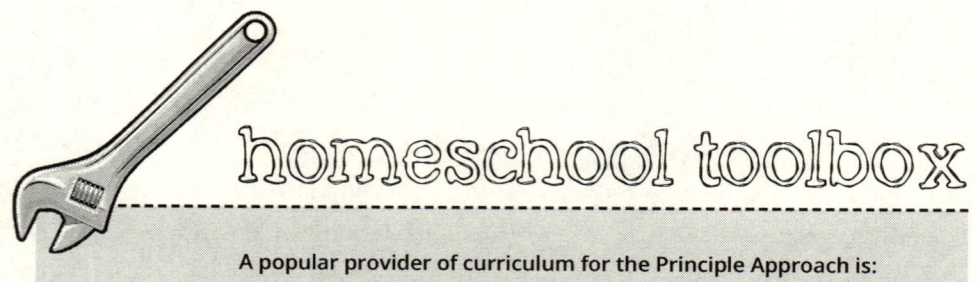

A popular provider of curriculum for the Principle Approach is:
➤ The Noah Plan – face.net

Montessori Style

Dr. Maria Montessori, a physician and educator from Italy, developed the Montessori style of education during the late 1800s and early 1900s. She believed in respecting the individual needs of children by allowing them to learn at their own pace and in their own way, leading to happy and confident children. One of the main expressions of a Montessori education is fostering independence in children in everything from education to life skills. One of the ways to attain good habits of independence is through repetition, or opportunities to practice skills until they are mastered. Other aspects particular to a Montessori education include cultural awareness, science and art experiences, and plenty of materials, supplies, and books at the ready for the child. The most interesting part of this style is that children are not required to do any school work. The parent is to make suggestions and give guidance, but never force learning upon the child. It's believed that showing respect and kindness will be enough encouragement for the child to become interested in one or more of the many opportunities awaiting him. The parent is simply supposed to keep detailed records of what the child actually does, rather than lesson plans. Finally, use of electronics such as the television are frowned upon (The International Montessori Index, n.d.; Montessori Mom, n.d.).

Advantages of the Montessori Method

- ✓ Self-starters who love to learn in their own way will thrive in this situation.
- ✓ Children can work at their own level because graded materials aren't used.
- ✓ It builds self-confidence and independence.
- ✓ The parent must simply make sure there are plenty of learning opportunities in the form of art supplies, science experiment supplies, history books, field trip options, and so on available to the child and needn't worry too much about preplanning.

- ✓ Learning through play is encouraged.
- ✓ It can be very hands-on for the child.

Disadvantages of the Montessori Method

- ✗ The parent doesn't get to be in complete control because this style is very child-centered.
- ✗ There is potential for major academic gaps in learning.
- ✗ Children who are unmotivated will likely become lax in their studies.
- ✗ Children who have a hard time making decisions will likely be frustrated.
- ✗ Some of the approved Montessori materials can be expensive; however, they aren't necessary.

Two how-to books written by Elizabeth G. Hainstock are available to help you learn more about this style: *Teaching Montessori in the Home: The Pre-School Years* and *Teaching Montessori in the Home: The School Years*.

Two popular providers of Montessori curriculum include:
- ▸ Montessori Environments – michaelolaf.com
- ▸ Shiller Math – shillermath.com

Unschooling

Unschooling can best be described as getting an education without "doing" school. Unschooling families make this happen in various ways, but some commonalities among most unschoolers is education that is fueled by the interests of the child, learning that flows naturally with real-life, and very few must-do lessons assigned by the parents. It's assumed that learning occurs in a rather organic way as children go about life, and that even simple tasks involve many academic opportunities (Unschooling.com, n.d.).

Advantages of Unschooling

- ✓ Children who thrive when learning by the beat of their own drum will likely enjoy the freedom of unschooling.
- ✓ Children find that life is learning, promoting a life-long love of learning.
- ✓ It's a rather stress-free method of learning.
- ✓ School and real life are one in the same, relieving some family time constraints.
- ✓ There are no lessons for the parent to plan; however, the parent certainly must nurture the child's curiosity and provide an atmosphere full of opportunities.

Disadvantages of Unschooling

- ✗ Children who are unmotivated to learn, explore, play creatively, and so on might not make the best use of all the free time.
- ✗ Parents who struggle with discipline issues will probably struggle even more with this ultra-relaxed approach to learning.
- ✗ Even though there will be gaps in any education, including public and private schools, unschooling presumably leaves many gaps, considering that a child learns only what he really wants to learn.
- ✗ Children who aren't following a plan for learning at least similarly to that of the public schools might have some trouble reentering school at grade level should it become necessary.

Some popular how-to books about unschooling include *The Unschooling Handbook: How to Use the Whole World as Your Child's Classroom* by Mary Griffith and any book by John Holt.

Because unschoolers don't rely on any set curriculum, there are no popular curriculum providers to list. That doesn't mean unschoolers never use curriculum, though. If a child is interested in learning about the Revolutionary War, for instance, a textbook might be the mode of education that is decided upon.

Accredited Curriculum

Essentially, with accredited curriculum you act as the teacher, while the providing school acts as the assessor and record keeper. Curriculum can come in many forms from textbooks, to CD-ROMs, to DVD or Internet classes. The child completes the work at home with the parent as the overseer. Sometimes, online or phone support from a teacher is available. Once the work is completed, quizzes, tests, and other assignments are sent into the school for grading. They keep a record of grades for your child, and prepare report cards, transcripts, and diplomas.

Advantages of Accredited Schools

- ✓ The providing schools do all the grading and record keeping for you. You don't even have to design high school transcripts.
- ✓ All the curriculum choices are made for you and all subjects are thoroughly covered.
- ✓ Some of these schools offer a high school graduation ceremony if that's important to you.
- ✓ There is little planning to do on the part of the parent because lessons are very scheduled and most material comes from textbooks.
- ✓ Many accredited schools offer curriculum in a variety of formats including textbooks, DVD lessons, and/or computerized lessons.
- ✓ Sometimes, your child will have phone or online chat access to teachers or tutors for questions.

Disadvantages of Accredited Schools

- ✗ The schedule is very rigid and doesn't allow for freedom to pursue deep interests in learning.
- ✗ If a particular subject isn't working for your child, you may not be allowed other choices.
- ✗ The services of the schools can be very expensive.
- ✗ Many of the services the schools provide are not difficult to complete at home, and may, in fact, cause you a little more work than if you kept up with the grading and recording yourself.

homeschool toolbox

There are more accredited schools than I even know about, so there's no way I can give you a complete listing. I have included a list of some of those that are widely known and respected below.

- ▸ Calvert School – homeschool.calvertschool.org
- ▸ Grace Academy – thegraceacademy.org
- ▸ Jubilee Academy – thejubileeacademy.org
- ▸ Keystone School – keystoneschoolonline.com
- ▸ Laurel Springs School – laurelsprings.com

Distance Learning

Unlike most accredited schools, distance learning allows you to take only the number of classes you desire. Depending on who offers the classes, they might be self-paced, teacher-led via the Internet, or you might actually travel some distance to attend an intensive class in a camp-like atmosphere.

Advantages of Distance Learning

- ✓ Courses are taught by someone other than the parent.

- ✓ Courses can often be independently completed by the student.
- ✓ One or two courses can be integrated into other homeschooling styles easily.
- ✓ Many challenging classes are available to meet exceptional needs.
- ✓ They can be a very convenient way to fulfill a requirement or interest when you lack resources nearby.
- ✓ Some distance-learning options provide phone or online support.
- ✓ Parents can use distance-learning courses to supplement a subject area in which they lack knowledge or expertise.

Disadvantages of Distance Learning

- ✗ Courses can be expensive.
- ✗ If a child isn't motivated or responsible enough to keep up with a self-paced program, it could be hard for him to complete work on time.
- ✗ With some programs, high speed Internet is necessary, you must be home at certain times for online classes, or you must make travel plans.
- ✗ The parent may still have to be the tutor on occasion.
- ✗ Most distance-learning classes specifically for gifted and talented children will require test scores and/or applications.
- ✗ Some programs have a limited number of courses in each subject area.

homeschool toolbox

Although many universities and community colleges across the nation offer distance-learning courses, I want to focus more specifically on a few of the many programs that are geared directly toward distance learning for gifted and talented children. This is not an exhaustive list. You can find other colleges by typing "gifted talented distance learning" into your Internet search engine.

- Institute for Mathematics and Computer Science – eimacs.com
- Johns Hopkins University's Center for Talented Youth – cty.jhu.edu
- Northwestern University's Center for Talented Development – ctd.northwestern.edu

Cottage Schools

Although particular cottage schools vary, most offer a classroom setting once or twice a week where your child receives instruction by certified or noncertified teachers. Assignments are given to be completed at home during the remainder of the week. Although it's still considered homeschooling because the child is at home more than she is in the classroom, the parent is not preparing assignments or choosing curriculum. He simply makes sure the assignments are completed for the cottage school.

There are a large variety of cottage schools throughout the United States. However, Classical Conversations is an example of a program that is nationwide. You can learn more about their program by visiting classicalconversations.com.

Advantages of Cottage Schools

- ✓ The parent is not responsible for planning the coursework or lessons for the particular subjects taught by the cottage school.
- ✓ Subject areas or topics that some parents dread are usually offered through cottage schools.

- ✓ One or more teachers are available in and often out of class for questions.
- ✓ The child gets to experience a classroom setting and have regular social contact.
- ✓ The child is accountable to someone other than the parent for completion of work and test taking.

Disadvantages of Cottage Schools

- ✗ Although the parents is still home with the child several days per week, he is not "the" teacher, but is still responsible more making sure the child understands the work and completes it.
- ✗ There can be quite a lot of homework assigned, leaving little time for personal interests.
- ✗ Children who did not or would not respond well in a regular classroom setting may struggle in this setting as well.
- ✗ Cottage schools can be quite expensive.

Cooperatives

Homeschooling cooperatives (co-ops) are formal and informal groups of homeschooling families who work together to offer classes to their children. They are meant for supplementation to your own homeschool. Depending on the group, they might meet twice a week, once a week, or even less. Quite often, parents with various talents or experiences teach classes while the other parents help out in other ways such as managing younger children or cleaning up the space after class. More formal co-ops will sometimes hire specialized teachers to come in for a fee.

Co-ops are located in almost every area of the Unites States. You can find one by searching your state's homeschool support group's website. If you can't find a co-op nearby, they are relatively easy to start. I've provided detailed how-to information in Chapter 8.

Advantages of Cooperatives

- ✓ Co-ops often offer classes that are best taught in group settings like debate, chess, and cooperative games.
- ✓ Oftentimes, the group can purchase supplies together that would be very expensive to purchase individually. For example, the families involved in a biology dissection class can each pay a fee to buy several dissection specimens for the class. The students will experience far more dissection opportunities as compared to spending the same money in their individual homeschools.
- ✓ Co-ops allow you to lean on the strengths of others while still maintaining your role as the main teacher of you homeschool.
- ✓ They allow for social interaction on a regular basis.
- ✓ Because the parents are usually expected to help even if they are not teaching, co-ops are nice for parent socialization as well.

Disadvantages of Cooperatives

- ✗ Depending on the group, co-ops can cost money.
- ✗ It takes time from you week to be part of the co-op.
- ✗ The parent is usually expected to help in some capacity.
- ✗ Sometimes classes aren't quite what you expected and can be either too hard or too easy.
- ✗ You might occasionally run into frustrating social interactions.

Eclectic Homeschooling

This is the style many families choose rather than pinning themselves to one of the particular methods previously mentioned. Quite simply, parents pick and choose what works best for each situation. During the course of a year, for instance, your child might use a traditional textbook curriculum for math and language arts and unit studies for history and science, incorporating Charlotte

Mason style short lessons and a Montessori life skills approach. I don't tell you this to confuse you, but encourage you that it's okay to mix and match to best benefit your child.

> **homeschool hint**
>
> Don't expect to find your perfect homeschooling niche right away. It generally takes 2 or 3 years of trial and error to find a groove that works for both you and your child. This doesn't mean the first years are wasted! You both will be learning together and your time will still be fruitful. It simply might take a little while to find the method(s), curricula, and daily schedule that fit your family perfectly.

Is Homeschooling Legal?

When considering which type of homeschool you want to have, it's very important to consider the laws and regulations of your state. In my state of Kentucky, I'm very lucky to have quite a lot of leeway in how I homeschool. As long as I teach certain subjects over the course of a defined number of days, I'm free to choose how to do that without asking anyone's permission. In other words, I don't have to report or defend my curriculum choices, or explain why I might be using several grade levels for various subjects with the same child.

Not all states are as permissive as mine. Some states will require you to follow certain certified curriculum, while others ask you to present your own choices for approval. Some states will even expect to see documentation in various forms to prove you have schooled your children appropriately during the school year.

To make sure you're following all the legal requirements of your state, I highly suggest you visit the Homeschool Legal Defense Association's (HSLDA) website: hslda.org. On this site, you can find a listing of homeschool laws for every state and territory of the United States. HSLDA is a wonderful nationwide advocate of homeschooling. It provides links to every state's regulations as well as offers answers to many questions people have about the legalities of homeschooling.

homeschool hint

As a side note, I highly encourage you to become a member of HSLDA. For a small yearly fee, you will have 24-hour access to a homeschooling attorney who will answer your questions and represent your family if a legal issue regarding homeschooling should ever arise. They also fight vehemently around the world for the right to homeschool, which your yearly dues help to support.

Depending on each state's requirements, you will be given a framework of sorts that will tell you:

- how many hours or days you must teach for the completion of a full school year,
- what subjects you must cover,
- how you should keep records,
- whether or not you must give your children achievement tests, and
- what accountability steps you must take.

If you live in a state that is fairly rigid in its requirements, I'd like to be the first to encourage you to think outside the box to meet the needs of your gifted child. I'm not suggesting that you disregard the rules, but I am saying there are sometimes creative ways to fulfill the rules. We are talking about homeschooling children who are exceptional, right? So, they deserve an exceptional education that puts fewer limitations on their potential.

Let me explain with an example. If my state says I have to teach one hour of history a day, I don't take that to mean that my children have to sit at a desk reading a history text and filling out history papers until the egg timer goes off one hour later. Although textbooks and worksheets can be part of our history studies, so can DVDs, field trips, walks through the historical part of town, recipes from a certain time period, historical fiction, classes at the history museum, parades celebrating history, art and craft projects, creating historical models, Internet research, historical board games, and the list goes on. If your state doesn't absolutely require the completion of certain material, let your child's interest and zeal take him to the moon.

As another example, many gifted children need to work in their own way. If a child wants to immerse herself into a history project all day for 2 weeks straight and then not touch the topic of history again for several weeks, that's okay. In one day's time, she's probably covered the required hours of history for an entire week or more. By the end of 2 weeks, she will have compiled nearly half a year's worth of history! Your job as teacher will be making sure all the subjects are covered, not necessarily when and in what order.

Personally, I have a "school is life and life is school" philosophy that really helps me let go of the thought that I have to check off each and every hour of each and every subject before I can rest my head at night. My children are expected to complete formal lessons daily, but they're also given a fair amount of productive free time in which to pursue interests. Music lessons, horse training, knitting and sewing, cooking and baking, and nature study have all come from those "idle" hours. In addition, I have no problems counting things like horse training and nature study towards science hours. I really encourage you to think about your child's educational needs and his day as a whole when you start fulfilling your state's requirements. Obey the rules, but use them in ways that benefit your child.

AN OVERVIEW OF HOMESCHOOLING

Where Do I Start?

I'll give you a general step-by-step for getting started with homeschooling, but I strongly encourage you to search online for the name of a homeschool leader in your area who is willing to talk you through getting started. It's so very encouraging to have a confident voice on the other end of the phone who can answer all your local questions.

1. Generally, the first place to start is to learn your state's requirements. You'll want to keep a binder of important homeschool documents, beginning with a copy of the requirements where you have highlighted pertinent parts.
2. The second step is to come up with a plan. Who will stay home with your child? Who will teach each subject? How will you organize your day? What curriculum will you use? Will you take any outside classes? Keep a list of your tentative plans in your binder.
3. Next you'll want to notify your school board if that's a requirement in your state. Keep any documentation the school gives you.
4. If your school board requires anything from you such as a written plan, supply it in a timely fashion. Keep a copy for yourself and any documentation the school board gives you.
5. Order your curriculum. Don't go overboard – you can spend a lot of money fast. Choosing curriculum will get easier the longer you homeschool, so don't be afraid to make changes once you realize something isn't working.
6. Get started! Don't try to jump into everything the first day. Take it slowly, adding a new subject once you feel comfortable with the first.

homeschool hint

Most homeschoolers who quit, do so the first year because they try to replicate school at home. They try to complete every subject every day, spending way too much time with busywork just to fulfill those hourly requirements. Have a place for your child to do schoolwork, but allow him the freedom to move around, take breaks, and set some of his own course.

Classroom students only sit in desks, have hour-long classes, and scheduled breaks to maintain order. You aren't trying to maintain order; you are trying to create an atmosphere of excitement and opportunities for learning!

While I'm on the subject, children who have previously been in the classroom require a measurable amount of transition time. They may balk about homeschooling for some time, saying things about missing friends, the predictability, and how much easier the work was. Be understanding, but firm in your decision to homeschool. If you waffle about the decision, the transition time will only last much longer, making both of you miserable. Instead, be sure school time is pleasant. Spend a lot of time immersing your child in subjects and projects she enjoys. Get involved in homeschooling groups, clubs, and classes that will keep her from feeling lonely. Before you know it, she'll be wondering why she ever wanted to go back to the classroom in the first place!

Where Do I Find Support and How Can I Be a Better Teacher?

All homeschool parents need support, especially in the beginning. You need other parents to learn from and talk to who understand your unique needs, especially when homeschooling gifted kids. Parents without support rarely stick with homeschooling for the long haul because they burn out or begin to doubt themselves. Luckily, homeschooling is a very popular option, meaning local support groups can be found in just about every area across the United

AN OVERVIEW OF HOMESCHOOLING

States. Groups will vary in style, but almost always offer at least some network of support for the parent.

Some groups will specifically have parents in mind and will host classes, friendship-building events, discussion groups, and more to build homeschooling confidence and offer you a time to talk and listen. Other groups will be more centered on your children and their needs, but will still offer you opportunities for socializing and learning with other parents. Either way, you'll find this support invaluable!

homeschool hint

Even though I went into homeschooling with a master's degree in education and experience in teaching, my support group kept me aflaot those first few years. My family has constantly been involved in one or more support groups from the beginning. They are good for my children and keep me motivated.

Just like public and private school teachers complete classes of continuing education, it's wise for you to take time to learn more about your job as a homeschool teacher. There are more opportunities to do this than you might think! Some of the local support groups that I mentioned above will have training workshops weekly, monthly, or quarterly where veteran homeschoolers will teach you everything from how to help struggling readers, to creating an exciting learning atmosphere, to dealing with discipline issues.

Annual homeschooling conventions are another source of encouragement and training. In almost every state across the country, you will find at least one homeschool convention within driving distance during the spring or summer seasons. Well-known speakers and curriculum providers gather to offer you a tremendous amount of expertise and advice. I have been attending conferences from the very beginning of our homeschool career and always leave feeling refreshed and motivated.

Online conferences allow you to attend homeschool workshops from the comfort of your home. Well-seasoned speakers present workshops via the Internet and you simply listen to the presentations you're most interested in. Typically, recordings of each session are made available after any conference for you to purchase and listen to again if you like.

Homeschool podcasts are numerous these days. They can give you bursts of encouragement and training while you fold the laundry or walk on the treadmill. Simply search "homeschooling" in your favorite podcast app to find an incredible array of episodes and topics to meet your needs.

Being part of a local or state support group will be important for finding out about local, state, and online opportunities for seminars, as well as curriculum sales, field trip opportunities, and more.

Now that you know the basics of getting started with homeschooling, let's talk about curriculum choices!

chapter 3

Choosing Curriculum

What Do You Have to Teach?

This chapter sets out to encourage you to design a homeschool structure that really meets the needs of your gifted child. Before diving into what you might include in that structure, though, you need to be able to answer the question, "What do I *have* to teach?"

Each state has its own requirements about what must be taught in the homeschool. As I mentioned in the last chapter, my state of Kentucky is very lenient. I'm given a total number of days which I must teach, a total number of hours that constitute a day's worth of school, and a listing of subjects that must be covered. From that point, I'm free to choose whatever curricula and learning methods that I like. Other states are far less lenient. Some even insist that curriculum must be purchased from one of a few acceptable choices or must be approved by someone in the state's education department.

Because fifty states equal almost fifty different regulations, I don't want to offer specifics about what you have to teach. Every state should have a statewide homeschool support group that offers a printable set of regulations on its website. If you have trouble locating your state's support group, visit HSLDA (hslda.org).

homeschool hint

Be sure to keep the legalities of your state in mind as you consider curriculum choices.

Choosing Curriculum for Various Learning Styles

From the previous chapter, you have an idea of the various homeschooling methods. Before choosing any particular method, and eventually curriculum, it's very important to consider your child's learning style(s). Learning styles are the approaches to learning that your child prefers and through which he learns best.

In 1983, Harvard professor Howard Gardner developed his theory of multiple intelligences which designates eight distinct modalities of learning (see Table 5; Gardner, 1998/2004; Gardner, 2005; Robinson, Shore, & Enersen, 2007). He stated that everyone learns best through one or more of these modalities, and therefore should be offered opportunities to do so.

Most school programs cater to the linguistic and logical/mathematical styles, which can mean those who excel in other styles can be left out or labeled as having learning difficulties or other learning issues like ADHD. As homeschoolers, we have two distinct advantages:

1. We know our children and can better pinpoint their learning styles.

Table 5. Learning Styles Based on Howard Gardner's Theory of Multiple Intelligences

Linguistic	These children enjoy and easily use words. They like to read, play word games, write stories, listen to lectures, and can usually express themselves well.
Logical / Mathematical	These children can reason well and work easily with numbers. They are able to think abstractly and enjoy mysteries, logic, experiments, patterns, and problem solving.
Bodily / Kinesthetic	These children use their bodies in almost everything they do. They prefer to learn while being active or in a hands-on way. You will often find them touching things, making things, and using body language when they speak.
Musical	These children love music and rhythm and respond well to learning that involves those things. On the other hand, they can also be very sensitive to noise that surrounds them and often prefer to have subtle background noise to keep focused.
Spatial	These children are daydreamers, artists, chart and map makers, and enjoy learning though pictures, diagrams, and visual media.
Naturalist	These children are very aware of their physical surroundings and are very good a defining and recognizing changes in the weather, flora, and fauna.
Interpersonal	These children love to interact with others. They are your social butterflies and prefer learning in groups.
Intrapersonal	These children prefer to learn alone. They are generally very reflective and have a strong sense of what they stand for, which makes them uneasily swayed by others.

(Infed, 2008 & Wikipedia, n.d.)

2. We have the wonderful opportunity to choose schooling methods and curriculum to perfectly meet the needs of our children.

The first step, then, would be identifying a child's learning styles. Careful observation will help you make some assessments, while inventories can help you make definite judgments. Learning style inventories can be purchased or taken for free on the Internet. Once you have a good idea of your child's learning style(s), it might be helpful to read about how to best teach towards that style.

homeschool toolbox

A few good books for identifying and teaching toward specific learning styles include:

- *The Way They Learn: How To Discover and Teach to Your Child's Strengths* by Cynthia Ulrich Tobias
- *The Big What Now Book of Learning Styles: A Fresh and Demystifying Approach* by Carol Barnier
- *Discover Your Child's Learning Style: Children Learn in Unique Ways — Here's the Key to Every Child's Learning Success* by Mariaemma Willis and Victoria Kindle Hodson.

Knowing your child's learning style before you choose curriculum will allow you to make better decisions from the start, rather than wasting time and money on products that don't work. Along the same lines, I highly recommend that you visit a homeschool convention or view several curriculum samples to familiarize yourself with some curriculum possibilities before purchasing. You'll know quickly which materials will and will not meet your needs once you're able to browse through them.

How Do You Design Your Own Curriculum Plan?

All children excel at some things more than others, and this is definitely true of gifted kids. A parent might notice that her child is a whiz at math and science, on grade level for history and reading, but struggling with grammar, spelling, and writing. She knows without a doubt that a pre-packaged curriculum on her child's grade level will be way too easy in some subjects and way too hard in others. In this instance, the child will benefit most from educational choices on various grade levels, which means a pre-packaged curriculum isn't the best option. But, with all the product choices available, how is a parent supposed to put together an appropriate and thorough curriculum plan on her own?

The answer begins again with looking at your state's educational requirements. Once you see, for example, that a fourth grader in your state is required to study math, reading, grammar, spelling, writing, physical science, state history, and an intro to foreign language, you'll have your starting point.

Next, you take into account your child's approximate grade level for each subject. If you have no idea what grade level your child is working on, there are online assessment tests available for free. For example, I use Saxon Math by John Saxon with my children. Saxon offers a free placement test online so I can determine the book level in which my children should be working. I don't worry about their age or grade, I simply use the book which is on their current ability level. Conducting Internet searches such as "free math placement test" and "determining reading level" should help you find sources for placement tests, or at least grade level approximations.

Remember that almost every single textbook builds in a thorough review of concepts taught in previous years. When questioning which grade level to buy, I tend to err on the side of a higher level knowing there will be review from the lower level if we need it. The only time I err on the side of the lower level is when I feel like a child has missed very important fundamental concepts and cannot move on without a thorough understanding.

homeschool hint

One note of caution, just because your gifted child might be able to solve algebraic equations, build a solar powered car and name every President of the United States at the age of six, doesn't mean he should skip the "basics". Be very sure your child completely grasps the fundamentals of all math functions, for instance, before deciding he should jump right into a math curriculum that is years beyond his age. Phonics and math are two subjects where understanding fundamentals is of utmost importance before moving on.

Once you know what the state expects and have approximate grade levels at which your child is working, the final step in choosing curriculum is to consider your child's learning style(s). Let's say you know your fourth grader needs a basic math course and is working on a fifth grade level. You find five different choices for fifth grade math curriculum, but know your child is a bodily-kinesthetic learner. Taking cost into consideration, you will want to purchase the curriculum that offers lots of hands-on learning with math manipulatives to teach the concepts.

As another example, let's say you have a seventh grader who is a voracious reader, but prefers literature over textbooks. Your state requirements say you must cover ancient history during the seventh grade year, and you've located four curriculum choices that are appropriate for grades 7-12. Two of the curricula offer a textbook/worksheet approach, one offers a literature-based/essay approach, and one offers a hands-on project approach. Which one should you choose? Obviously, your voracious reader will most prefer the literature-based/essay approach because she gets to learn doing what she loves most – reading good literature.

Subject by subject, you think through what your state requires, what grade level you need to find, and what type of curriculum would best meet your child's learning style(s). Before you know it, you've designed your own curriculum plan! What's even more exciting (if you don't wait until the last minute and make wise choices) is that designing your own curriculum plan usually costs far less than purchasing a pre-packaged curriculum.

How Can You Make Curriculum Work for Your Child?

It's possible that sometimes you'll be stuck with a curriculum that isn't perfect for your child. Maybe you're strapped monetarily and have been given hand-me-down curriculum from a friend, or maybe you've tried several things and nothing seems to be "just right". There's no need to worry. Another beauty of homeschooling is that you can tweak any program to meet your needs. Let me give you some examples.

The Science Textbook Doesn't Go as Deep as Your Child Is Capable

You have several choices for a very easy fix. Go to the library for additional books on the topic or find a safe website for your child to read in addition to or in place of the text. Give your child a research project in which she must find more information about the topic herself. Or, assign her an additional experiment or hands-on project to show her in-depth understanding of the topic.

You'll be excited to know that adding research projects, experiments, and hands-on activities is not as hard as it might seem. There are tons of free, creative ideas on the Internet. Simply doing a quick online search of your topic will give you book lists, websites, and directions for experiments and projects.

real-life example

> After reading a chapter in a science text about the reproduction of flowers, my kids needed more. We printed a chart from the Internet of the parts of a flower and headed outdoors to collect various flower samples. Upon returning home, we dissected the flowers, drew the parts, and used the chart to help us label our drawings.
>
> Later, I checked out from the library an illustration-rich, non-fiction book about flower reproduction. Again, we headed outside to find flowers in various stages of reproduction and noted these in our science journals. Rather than offer the boring test from the science text, I asked my children to work together to reenact the process of flower reproduction in a skit.

The Spelling Curriculum Is Way Too Advanced for Your Child

Again, you have many options besides purchasing a new curriculum. My first suggestion is always to take a step back and evaluate if there's anything in the curriculum that your child can handle. If so, go back to that point and start again s-l-o-w-l-y. There is no curriculum rule that says your child must complete one page per day or one lesson per week. Yes, the books are set up so that you will have lessons to take you through an entire year's worth of school days, but it won't help your child to progress at that pace if he can't handle it. You'll actually do far more good for your child to begin again at a pace that's suitable.

As you begin again slowly, be sure he fully comprehends the concept before moving on to anything new. Think back to the learning style(s) you recognized in your child and try to implement some of those strategies. If your child is a musical learner, for instance, it might help to put a spelling rule to music, chant, or rhythm. If he is a kinesthetic learner, he might simply need to spell words as he tosses a ball – one letter per toss.

Occasionally, a text will actually be too advanced and you have little choice but to go back one grade level or more. If this is necessary, don't allow your child to feel bad about the setback. It's reasonable to assume that going back to the point of misunderstanding and relearning concepts using correct learning styles will allow him to catch up quickly.

real-life example

> Spelling hasn't been the easiest of subjects for my son. I bounced from one curriculum to the next thinking that something would surely work. None of them did. He would make small strides, but nothing measurable. Then it clicked that the problem didn't have anything to do with the order of the spelling skills or the amount of practice for a list of words. It was that my son is highly creative and loves to be active in learning.
>
> Using one of the many spelling prorams now sitting on the bookshelf, I started over again. This time, I made sure to take extra time with each lesson to incorporate creative and active lessons. We wrote spelling words on the sidewalk with chalk, in shaving cream spread all over the table, and using magnet letters. We practiced spelling words while doing jumping jacks and shooting basketballs. We made a spelling rule chart that took up the better portion of a wall so that he could add to the wall each time we learned a new rule. Backing up to redo the lessons in a way that met him where he was made all the difference.

The History Curriculum Is Strictly Textbook Reading with Paper and Pencil Tests, But Your Child Really Needs Something Hands-On to Make Connections

With a small amount of effort on your part, this problem is easy to fix, too. To add hands-on activities to a lesson, all you'll need is a source for ideas. A quick Internet search will turn up plenty of ideas, but your library will have books that offer activity ideas on particular subjects, too. If the history text is covering the topic of Ancient Rome, do a quick search to find the "Juvenile Ancient Rome" books at your library. A quick scan of the shelves should turn up at least one book full of age-appropriate, hands-on activity ideas.

Obviously, this takes a little preparation on your part because you'll not only need to find the ideas, but gather materials as well. Some parents don't enjoy the effort (and occasional mess) of hands-on projects, but for children whose learning depends on them, it's worth the effort.

real-life example

> I owned a b-o-r-i-n-g textbook on the subject of early American history. Even I would almost fall asleep when we pulled it out for a lesson. I didn't have the extra money to buy better curriculum, but I knew that I didn't want my children to see the rich and wonderful history of the birth of our nation as tiresome and unimportant. So, off to the library I went.
>
> I ended up checking out three wonderful books that day. One was a highly illustrated nonfiction book about the era; another was a book full of hands-on activities to make the era come to life; and the third was an historical fiction book that set us right in the time period beautifully.
>
> By ditching the boring textbook completely, our time exploring early American history quickly became exciting. We made models, dressed in period costumes, reenacted battles, constructed toys, baked yummy treats, produced crafts of the period, and more.
>
> At the end of the study, instead of assigning a test, I asked my kids to create a poster report depicting everything they had learned. They still remember wonderful facts about early American history today, and I'm sure this wouldn't have been the case if we had stuck with the original textbook.

The Language Arts Curriculum Adds Way Too Many Hands-On Activities and Your Child's Learning Is Distracted by Them

This is perhaps the easiest fix of all. Ditch the hands-on activities! Just because a curriculum offers the extra ideas, doesn't mean you have to use them. Linguistic and logical/mathematical children are often bothered by the extras and their learning can actually be hindered.

real-life example

> When my daughter reached high school, she transitioned into textbooks more often than in previous years. Because she had spent so many years prior doing hands-on science, we found that she had already conducted many of the experiment suggestions in her science textbooks. She felt it was quite worthless to do the same experiments over again and I agreed. As long as she could correctly explain the outcome to me, I allowed her to skip it and move on.

You Like the Content of the Science Curriculum, But Your Child Wants to Take Rabbit Trails

Many gifted children like learning on their own terms and want to stray from the material in a textbook for that reason alone. Others are so often intrigued by a topic that they want to learn more or take the focus in a different direction than the text. I feel like I keep saying this, but that's another huge advantage of homeschooling. You aren't tied to the text.

In my home, the text often serves as the syllabus rather than the learning material. In other words, the text gives me the important topics that need to be covered. We may use the textbook lessons as a starting point, but never fear going off in our own direction if either my children or I see fit. I make the "syllabus" clear at the beginning of the year and tell my children, "These are the things we have to cover at some point this year. It's okay with me if we use something other than the textbook to cover some of the topics, and it's okay with me if we study additional topics. However, the school year won't be considered final until these topics have been covered in one way or another."

With gifted kids, two of my best tools are organization and expectations. I plan our general school year during the summer, but leave the specifics to work out as the year progresses. During the summer, I will plan the basic topics that need to be covered for each subject and the main texts or materials we'll use. As the school year begins, I show my children the main materials and outline the topics that must be covered. My organization allows them clear expectations for the year ahead. We can then dive into learning with some freedom about how that learning will take place. In the end, my children feel an amount of freedom and independence, while staying within a reasonable framework at the same time.

real-life example

> During a study of oceans, my children learned the word biome and wanted to discover the other biomes of the world. This was not on my schedule. We needed to move on or all of my plans for the year would be ruined. Gasp!
>
> Being a brilliant homeschool mom, I knew how I could take care of this problem. We'd simply go check out a book from the library on biomes and nip this rabbit trail in the bud in a matter of the few minutes it would take to read the book.
>
> Ha! Little did I know that one book about biomes would only drive my children's interests further and further away from my schedule. In the end, my children created file folder reports on each and every biome, made fun snacks to represent each biome, learned about the characteristics of plants and animals within each biome, mapped every biome on a world map, and visited the zoo to categorize the animals into their appropriate biomes.
>
> Would you believe that I could never have planned such a wonderful study myself? And, would you believe that much of the information they learned during their interest-sparked study actually touched on some of the subjects in my plans that were left far behind? Yeah, homeschooling is pretty cool.

Should You Buy Curriculum or Create Your Own?

What if you find yourself making many, many adjustments to purchased curricula? Wouldn't it be easier and wiser to just write your own? That answers depends greatly on one main thing: your comfort level in writing curriculum. If you don't feel confident creating your own curriculum, it will probably be much easier to just keep making necessary adjustments to products you buy. However, if you have the confidence, go for it! Here's a quick step-by-step for writing your own material:

1. *Find at least one scope and sequence of the topic you're going to plan.* You might use the tables of contents from other curricula or search the Internet for key concepts. For example, if I'm planning a study of physical science for middle school, I'll see what some other texts include on the subject and I'll search the Internet for "key concepts physical science" or "physical science topics."

2. *Once you find the basic topics you need to cover, you'll think yet again about your child's learning style(s).* This will be the main element around which the course is planned. For example, if your child is spatial and interpersonal, you'll want to include plenty of opportunities for visual learning with charts, maps, and diagrams, as well as opportunities to learn alongside others sometimes.

> **homeschool hint**
>
> I don't want to give you the impression that your child can only learn in the mode of her learning style(s). Children need to be pushed outside of their comfort zones once in a while to complete assignments and activities that encourage new skills and stretch the mind. As we all know, life doesn't always allow us to live within our learning styles!

3. *The next step is to decide what the main method of learning about each topic will be.* Will you have your child read a library book about each concept, then complete some sort of paper or project? Will you give him lessons/lectures on the topic and then ask him to complete a worksheet you've created? Will you kick-off the lesson with an experiment or hands-on activity, then ask him to research the topic on the Internet and explain it to you? Will you take him on field trips to learn about the topic and ask him to keep a detailed field trip journal detailing all he's learned over the year? Or, will you do something a little different for each new topic? The choice is yours and the sky is the limit. It would be wise to include your child in some of this planning, especially if he likes to have some control over his own schooling.

4. *Finally, decide upon a schedule.* Do you want to allow your child to work freely through the curriculum? Would you like her to complete a certain part daily or weekly? Again, including your child in the planning will help her feel ownership in the work to be done.

When my oldest was in third grade, I wrote a grammar curriculum (West, 2009) for her to use because I couldn't find anything that "fit" during that stage of her learning. I'll share the process I used in creating that curriculum to give you a better idea of how I followed the steps above.

1. *Find at least one scope and sequence of the topic you're going to plan.* Quite simply, I did an online search for, "scope and sequence third grade grammar" and "scope and sequence fourth grade grammar." I jotted down the concepts taught by several reputable companies and developed my own list of what needed to be covered.
2. *Once you find basic topics you need to cover, you'll think yet again about your child's learning style(s).* My daughter, as I've told you, loves to read. I knew that I wanted to incorporate the reading of some really good literature into the program and that I wanted the grammar lessons to come from the literature. Because she excels linguistically, a simple explanation and short bursts of worksheet work would get the job done without wasting her time.
3. *The next step is to decide what the main method of learning about each topic will be.* Because the focus of these lessons was grammar, I chose to incorporate really good picture books that could be read in one sitting rather than longer chapter books. Then, she would complete small grammar and writing exercises that met one or more of the key concepts that I needed to cover. Additionally, I chose books from all genres to give her exposure to more than her usual reading interests.
4. *Finally, decide upon a schedule.* Since she enjoys working at her own pace, I designed the lessons so that she could finish one book's worth of activities on her own schedule. I set the boundary that each book and its grammar and writing lessons needed to be finished within one week. If she wanted to read the book and complete all the lessons in one day, that was fine with me. If she wanted to read the book one day and take a few days to complete all the lessons, that was also fine with me.

> **homeschool hint**
>
> Creating your own curriculum takes a little time, but the benefits can truly be worth it sometimes!

What If Your Child is Smarter Than You?

Believe it or not, this is a very legitimate concern with gifted kids! Some of them will be way beyond our level of understanding long before they leave our homeschools. Luckily for us, we aren't the only teaching resources our children have. In fact, our children have a vast array of resources simply because of the flexible environment homeschooling affords. And when you feel inadequate, don't be afraid to call in the bigger guns. Here are some ideas for finding help:

- Family members who work in a certain field and/or have expertise in a subject can be called on regularly.
- The same goes for friends. You just might not call quite as often so you don't wear out your welcome.
- More and more courses are becoming available online or via DVD so that the parent doesn't have to be an expert in every subject.
- Some areas host gifted homeschooling co-ops where kids can gather for classes with expert teachers.
- Community colleges are a great place for in-depth learning in a less-than-big-time-college atmosphere.
- Tutors can be hired in almost any subject. Look for a bright and eager college student who would love to talk tough subjects with your child.
- Some employers would love to mentor a bright child by allowing him to work alongside them.

- Don't forget the library and Internet contain wonderful answers to any question you or your child may have.

Celebrating Your Child's Passions

All children have passions, but gifted children's passions are often more obvious. Whether your child has a passion for ballet or violin, biology or volleyball, homeschooling allows him the extra time he needs to pursue his passion(s).

In reality, many homeschooling assignments can be completed in a relatively short amount of time. So, for example, when a child spends one hour in Spanish class at school, the actual work she completes is pretty comparable to what a child working at home can complete in about fifteen minutes. (I'm not talking about projects, but textbook work or worksheets.) When you think in those terms, you can imagine how homeschooling opens many hours for pursuing passions.

CHOOSING CURRICULUM

real-life example

In our own home, my daughter who loves horses, was afforded much time for her passion. Even in high school, she could typically finish most of her assigned schoolwork in three-five hours. Once finished, she spent time daily at the barn actually working with horses (and other animals) alongside her father and grandfather. She also hung out with the veterinarian when she came to call, helped the farrier, took part in the hay harvest, visited horse training centers, attended livestock auctions, and depleted the library of all their animal books. By the time she was a senior, she was interning on a thoroughbred horse farm and farm sitting for neighbors regularly. You won't be surprised that her passion went right along with her to college where she is getting a horse-related degree.

Additionally, our son began showing an interest in playing the guitar when he was about 12-years-old. Knowing nothing about guitar, we hired a local teacher for lessons. It wasn't long before that teacher was passing my son along to another teacher who could teach more difficult lessons. Again, it wasn't long before my son surpassed the second teacher. In total so far, we've been through five teachers. Besides his assigned practice, he has spent hours learning to play additional music and musical styles by ear or with the help of YouTube videos. He's taught himself crazy amounts of technology having to do with his craft, too. As a senior in high school, he plays lead guitar for four different churches, has made incredible connections in his field, and has aspirations to play in Nashville someday soon.

As you begin structuring your homeschool day, always remember to find time and opportunities to nurture your child's passions. Maybe he would like to be part of a chess or robotics club. Maybe he would like to have several hours to practice musical instruments weekly. Maybe he would like to have time to draw house plans, grow a garden, or create inventions. His best work will likely be done during these free times when he has the opportunity to chase his dreams.

As we move into chapter 4, we'll look in-depth at particular subject areas and how you can encourage your gifted or twice-exceptional learner's success in those areas.

chapter 4

Teaching All Learners

As you consider homeschooling methods and learning styles, you'll find the curriculum choices for each subject to be enormous and potentially overwhelming. In this chapter, I have suggested some options for various subjects for both those who excel and those who struggle. By no means are my suggestions your only options. Instead, I'm simply trying to get you headed in the right direction by including a few ideas and curriculum choices.

Reading

characteristics of a gifted reader

(Levand, 1999)

- Reads voraciously
- Reads well above grade level
- Comprehends well above grade level
- Often uses advanced vocabulary
- Often does well on tests

For Those Who Excel

My best advice for a child who excels in reading is to allow her to read as often as possible. Challenge her with plenty of classic literature and allow a healthy dose of books of her own choosing. Frequent trips to the library will keep your child and your wallet happy.

Children who love to read are typically able to absorb vast amounts of information through books. By encouraging non-fiction choices as well as really good fiction, especially historical fiction, you will be amazed at the understanding she gains in every subject.

Allowing your child to take part in a book discussion group through a library, homeschool group, or casual group of friends might be something a gifted reader would enjoy.

The classical education method mentioned in Chapter 2 offers a rigorous schedule of literature. Another very literature-rich curriculum choice would be Sonlight (sonlight.com). *Some of My Best Friends Are Books: Guiding Gifted Readers from Preschool to High School* by Judith Wynn Halsted is a great resource for your avid and advanced readers, too. An excellent curriculum to encourage higher order thinking skills along with reading comprehension from grades 1-9 is *Jacob's Ladder Reading Comprehension Program* by Joyce Van Tassel-Baska and Tamara Stambaugh.

Sometimes, children who are superb readers might not be up to the same level in writing just yet. To fill the gap, allow your child to do some assignments orally. For example, if a written book report wouldn't be in order, your child could draw a few scenes from the book and tell about it orally. You will encourage the excelled reading ability, comprehension, and in-depth thinking without building walls of frustration from a lack or writing skills.

homeschool toolbox

These websites offer wonderful book lists for gifted readers of all ages.
- Our Journey Westward – ourjourneywestward.com/living-literature
- 1000 Good Books List – classical-homeschooling.org/celoop/1000.html
- 101 Great Books Recommended for College-Bound Readers – hoagiesgifted.org/101_books_for_college_bound_readers.htm
- Association of Library Service to Children (a list of award winning books) – ala.org/alsc/awardsgrants/bookmedia/caldecottmedal/caldecotthonors/caldecottmedal
- Literature to Supplement History – da1.redshift.com/~bonajo/history.htm

For Those Who Struggle

It's difficult to give a conclusive fix for a child who struggles with reading because the problem could stem from so many different issues. If your child has never had a thorough course of phonics, you will most certainly want to start there. *Right Track Reading Lessons: A Highly Effective Step-by-Step Direct Systematic Phonics Program* by Miscese R. Gagen is one example of many products available for teaching phonics. I have chosen to include this curriculum as a suggestion because it can be used with multiple ages, whereas most phonics products are geared toward young children.

A child who is very slow and labored as she reads is often helped by reading books that are a grade or two lower than she is capable of reading. By reading books that are much easier, it allows your child to gain not only speed, but confidence in her reading ability.

Many issues, such as losing one's place while reading, not pausing for punctuations marks, and not reading with inflection, can be helped by simply having your child place a plain ruler or bookmark under the line she is reading to keep her mind focused on that line alone.

If reading comprehension is a problem, again, go back a grade level or two in reading. She should be expected to comprehend well only what she can read well. If she struggles with the actual mechanics of reading, she's probably not absorbing the material very well. Visuals can help your child understand the material. Ask her to draw a simple picture of what she's read. Help her think through details she's missing that can be added to the picture. Older children can make story maps by listing characters and their personalities or noting things about the plot or setting. A good place to find free blank story mapping pages is the Enchanted Learning website: enchantedlearning.com/graphicorganizers/storymap.

Some children who show signs of dyslexia, or those who continue to have problems even after concerted effort, might benefit from visual tracking exercises that train the eyes and brain to work better together. Your primary care physician or eye doctor can help you determine if this is a good option and where to go. Dianne Craft (diannecraft.org) has developed inexpensive materials especially for parents to use at home to help with such issues.

Many students with reading struggles respond well to audiobooks and/or eBooks. Both can be readily found in library systems, making them and economical choice, too.

Writing

characteristics of a gifted writer

(Peterson, 2006)

- Enjoys telling stories (fact or fiction) with lots of detail
- Has fun playing with words
- Writes more often and with more ability than children of the same age
- Can't wait to get thoughts on paper
- Is able to organize ideas easily
- Soaks up written or oral stories
- Expects others to show deep emotions in response to their writing
- Often loves reading finished writings aloud

For Those Who Excel

Let your child write! Writing takes time, so allow plenty of uninterrupted time. Although it's okay to give assignments, the best writing will come from topics and writing styles that inspire your child.

Make sure he has a good understanding of grammar, punctuation, and other writing practices. Luckily, most children who love to write naturally absorb the mechanics, but never be afraid to assign lessons to improve any area where his writing is lacking.

Provide your child with a wealth of rich material to read. The more he reads, the better examples he will have of what constitutes good writing. Consider filling his learning spaces with classic literature, fairy tales and fables, magazines, biographies, autobiographies, nonfiction books, reference books, poetry, and more. Don't forget to keep a dictionary and thesaurus nearby.

See if you can find a writing club through a local homeschool group or the library. Writing is always more fun when you have an audience. Speaking of audiences, let your child maintain a blog where he is the author and/or submit his writings to newspapers, magazines, and even publishers to see if they might be printed.

homeschool toolbox

Here is a small list of places that regularly publish writing from children.

- *Amazing Kids* Magazine – mag.amazing-kids.org
- *Cobblestone* and *Cricket* Magazines – cricketmedia.com/classroom/cobblestone-magazine
- *Creative Kids* Magazine – ckmagazine.org
- Figment – figment.com
- *Highlights for Children* Magazine – highlightskids.com
- Merlin's Pen: Fiction, Essays and Poems by America's Teens - merlynspen.org/us
- *Skipping Stones* Magazine – skippingstones.org
- *Stone Soup* Magazine – stonesoup.com
- *Teen Ink* Magazine – teenink.com

Has your avid writer ever thought about writing a novel? The National Novel Writing Month takes place every November (nanowrimo.org) and challenges participants to write a complete novel in one month's time. By registering on the website, your child has the opportunity to log his progress. Although there is no real pressure to actually finish the novel, the organization serves as an encourager and motivator.

Your young writer might like to join a few writing competitions, too. There are many to find through an online search of "writing competitions for kids." You could also check the Funds for Writers website (fundsforwriters.com/contests) to keep on top of writing competitions around the country.

homeschool toolbox

A few highly esteemed writing competitions include:

- Letters About Literature Contest – read.gov/letters
- National History Day Contest – nhd.org/national-contest
- Scholastic Art & Writing Competitions – artandwriting.org

Some fun curricula for writing projects include:

- *Learn to Write the Novel Way* by Carole Thaxton. By the end of this course, your child will have written his own complete novel.
- *One Year Adventure Novel* by Daniel Schwabauer. Upon completion of this course, your child will have written his own full adventure novel.
- *Write Your Roots* by Carole Thaxton and *Research and Writing: Activities that Explore Family History* by Douglas Rife. Through these books, your child will learn how to research and write about his genealogy.

For Those Who Struggle

Many times, writing is a struggle mostly because of the mechanics. It simply takes too long to write all of those wonderful thoughts. If this seems to be the case for your child, free his hands by allowing him to dictate his stories or other assignments once in a while. Dictation means you write or type the words your child speaks. He still comes up with the entire content and you can continue through the editing process with him, but you do the bulk of the writing/typing to free his mind. There are a variety of dictation apps available for download that can automate dictation for your children, too. Don't be afraid that writing independently will never happen. What you're actually doing is giving him a boost of confidence that there really are wonderful stories waiting to be told! Also, introduce a typing course early on to encourage him to recognize that physical writing isn't the only option.

Besides just being a slow writer, some children have difficulty with dysgraphia. If you notice letter and word reversals after the age of six, words written without spaces in between them, letters that seem to float above the line, and letters that are written from the bottom up, you might consider some simple training exercises offered by trained professionals. Dianne Craft (diannecraft.org), who I mentioned in the reading section, also offers at home dysgraphia exercises that can be easily implemented at home for improvement in writing. You might also consider a program called *Handwriting Without Tears* by Jan Olsen that offers multisensory, hands-on handwriting training that works well with children struggling with dysgraphia.

Some struggling writers do well when given prompts to set their imagination into action. A prompt can be a sentence, paragraph, or picture that helps your child find a beginning point for a story. A fun exercise to introduce the simplicity of continuing with a prompt is to tell stories orally with your child. You start telling a story, only to stop at an exciting or pivotal moment. Your child then takes over the oral story, adding his own flair. Once he understands the concept orally, it's an easy transition into written prompts. *Story Starters: Helping Children Write Like They've Never Written Before* by Karen Andreola is one book that offers a vast array of writing prompts already prepared for you.

homeschool hint

When my daughter struggled with finding writing topics and getting started, I made a set of story starters from magazines and calendar pictures. I simply cut out interesting pictures – a butterfly atop a toddler's hand, a woman standing at a door with a surprised look on her face, a rusty abandoned car – and glued them onto cardstock. I kept the picture cards in a folder labeled "writing inspiration." When she was stuck, she could grab a picture from the folder and develop a story with the photo as the main illustration.

Graphic organizers can be wonderful tools for struggling writers, too. These maps or charts allow a child to "see" his plan for writing. They can be used for any aspect of writing like brainstorming a topic, developing a plot, designing a setting, planning characters, and more. A software program called Kidspiration created by Inspiration Software (inspiration.com/Kidspiration) allows elementary children to create computerized visual organizers that smoothly transition into creative writing (and other subjects). Although the software is not wildly expensive, there are plenty of free graphic organizers available online as well.

homeschool toolbox

Take advantage of some of the many free graphic organizers that can be found on the internet.
- Ed Helper – edhelper.com/teachers/General_graphic_organizers.htm
- Enchanted Learning – enchantedlearning.com/graphicorganizers
- Houghton Mifflin English – eduplace.com/graphicorganizer

Try assigning various forms of writing to your children. You might be surprised that the same child who hates writing persuasive essays will flourish when allowed to write his own memoirs. Likewise, some kids just need a real-life experience to get motivated. Writing for publication or keeping a blog (both mentioned in the section for writers who excel) might help your child to become more prolific with writing.

Many writing curricula will walk your child step-by-step through various styles of writing. For instance, *Research in Increments: A Step-by-Step Guide to Writing Research Papers from a Christian Perspective* by Susan Kemmerer teaches the process of writing a thorough research paper over the course of several weeks. Each day, the author assigns only one new step of writing the paper and turns a potentially overwhelming project into a piece of cake.

homeschool toolbox

If your child needs some step-by-step writing instruction, you may find some of the following curricula helpful.

- *Jump In: A Workbook for Reluctant Writers* by Sharon Watson
- *Research in Increments: A Step-by-Step Guide to Writing Research Papers From a Christian Perspective* by Susan Kemmerer
- *Wordsmith* by Jane Cheaney
- *Writers in Residence* by Debra Bell
- *Writing Step-by-Step* by Mary Lou Ward

Another fun option is called the Stapleless Book (readwritethink.org/classroom-resources/student-interactives/stapleless-book-30010.html), a site where your child is prompted on the computer to write parts of a story using various templates provided. Once completed, the story is printed on one piece of paper that folds into a stapleless book. My less-than-zealous writer loves this site.

Grammar

characteristics of a child gifted in grammar, vocabulary, and/or spelling

- Tends to have a large vocabulary
- Often likes to read and/or write
- Often likes to speak
- Enjoys grammar, spelling, or vocabulary exercises
- May enjoy word puzzles
- Picks up on spelling or grammar rules very easily
- Often enjoys the challenge of another language

For Those Who Excel

Grammar is actually a very important subject to be purposely taught to those who excel in the language arts because understanding grammar always equals better writing and/or speaking skills. Also, grammar is closely tied to vocabulary. A strong mastery in both grammar and vocabulary corresponds to better test scores on the ACT, SAT, and achievement tests.

Oftentimes, when gifted kids "get" something, they don't like to keep practicing the same skill over and over again. Grammar is definitely one of those subjects where you can feel free to skip over some lessons or stop altogether once you find your student has absorbed the necessary information and uses it correctly day in and day out in his language and writing. In fact, there's a program that's perfect for gifted children that teaches grammar thoroughly and concisely only once in upper elementary school, then revisits it again in middle/early high school. With *Analytical Grammar: A Systematic Approach to Language Mastery* by R. Robin Finley and Erin Karl (analyticalgrammar.com), once the meaty, but compact, curriculum is completed, your bright child shouldn't need year after year of grammar lessons.

For Those Who Struggle

For children who struggle with grammar, the best approach is a slow and steady progression of lessons that systematically teach grammar rules. There are so many, many curriculum choices available that do this. Daily Grammar shares free online lessons that are succinct and thorough (dailygrammar.com/archive.html).

Spelling/Vocabulary

For Those Who Excel

With naturally gifted spellers you have two basic choices. First, you can continue offering spelling lessons that challenge your child and maybe even consider taking part in spelling bee competitions (spellingbee.com). Or, you can determine that you're pleased with her understanding and application of spelling and discontinue lessons. If you choose the latter, you might consider replacing spelling lessons with vocabulary building lessons. In doing so, either route you take – pursuing challenging spelling words or pursuing and expanded vocabulary – will broaden both your child's spelling and vocabulary skills. Spelling and vocabulary lessons are vastly available and each appeal to different learning styles. For this reason, I'll only mention one of each as recommended sources to get you started in your search for something wonderful. *Spelling Power* by Beverly L. Adams-Gordon is a self-paced curriculum appropriate for all age levels. *Wordly Wise 3000* by Kenneth Hodkinson and Sandra Adams is a comprehensive vocabulary program available for all grade levels.

Another option that actually continues to boost both spelling and grammar is to focus on learning another language (or two). Studying Latin and Greek exposes your child to the derivation of all modern languages, growing the understanding and vocabulary for all tongues. Additionally, children who have a background in Latin and Greek tend to score higher on tests because of their increased vocabulary. Also, consider the fields of work that require in-depth knowledge of Latin, Greek, or even Hebrew: doctors, veterinarians, nurses, pharmacists, chemists, researchers, lawyers, minsters, and more (Campbell, 2007).

Of course, Latin and Greek are not your only foreign language options. Learning any additional language will prove to broaden your child's education. Let her choose a culture of interest and begin learning the language along with other aspects of history, culture, economics, tourist's sites, and people. And think of how inspiring it would be to learn a language if you happen to be lucky enough to take a "field trip" to the native area!

homeschool toolbox

There are several companies who offer very good foreign language resources. I will list some of the most popular and let you peruse their websites to see if the targeted age and learning styles meet your needs.

- Classical Academic Press – classicalacademicpress.com
- Greek-N-Stuff – greeknstuff.com
- The Learnables – learnables.com
- Lively Latin – livelylatin.com
- Memoria Press – memoriapress.com
- Minimus – minimus-etc.co.uk
- Rosetta Stone – rosettastone.com

homeschool hint

Play games whenever you can! These fun language games will encourage a love for grammar, spelling, and/or vocabulary.

Apples to Apples	Bananagrams	Bookworm (video game)
Chunks	Cooking Up Sentences!	DICEcapades
Go to Press	Sentence Cube	Word Pirates
Smart Mouth	Spelling Beez	Sentence Says
You've Been Sentenced		Up for Grabs!

For Those Who Struggle

As with grammar, the best method for teaching spelling to struggling learners is to introduce rules in a slow and steady progression. I highly recommend using a prepared curriculum such as *All About Spelling* by Marie Ripple (a multisensory approach) or *Sequential Spelling* by Don McCabe. Both programs suggest that struggling spellers begin with Level 1 no matter their age, then progress through the levels as capable. For an older child who really only needs a quick overview or review of spelling rules and can then catch on pretty easily, I suggest *Apples: Daily Spelling Drills for Secondary Students* and *Apples 2: Daily Phonics Drills for Secondary Students* by Susan Kemmerer. One new spelling rule is introduced per week and then reviewed daily through fun crosswords and other puzzles to reinforce the rule.

Math

characteristics of a gifted mathematician

(Bossé & Rotigel, 2006)

- Learns math at a faster pace than peers
- Doesn't need much repetition to cement new concepts
- Is inquisitive about math (and often science)
- Often wants to know the "why" behind math concepts
- Isn't afraid to tackle math challenges
- Can become easily bored and frustrated with rote math or math below level
- May come up with creative ways to solve problems
- Enjoys math lessons, games, and puzzles relating to math

For Those Who Excel

Depending on the mathematical ability of your child, you have several options for meeting his needs. The easiest choice is to allow him to move through math materials at his own pace. If he understands a new concept and the next five lessons in the text review that concept, allow him to skip those five lessons. If you're absolutely sure skipping a grade level (or more) won't skip over fundamental concepts, go for it. As your child gets older, you will be able to offer him courses either through textbooks, online, or through local community colleges that cover topics that some students will never touch before graduation, such as calculus, trigonometry, statistics, or whatever his proposed interests desire.

For children highly gifted in math, John Hopkins Center for Talented Youth (cty.jhu.edu) offers online courses. For acceptance into this esteemed program, your child will need to go through an admissions process that requires the completion of one or more standardized tests.

Mathematically challenging curriculum can come in many forms besides skipping grade levels or taking specialized classes when you add plenty of logic and problem solving opportunities to round out the more technical side of the math textbook. Prufrock Press (prufrock.com) and Critical Thinking Press (criticalthinking.com) both offer wonderfully challenging materials to supplement math. Be sure to check out more about logic study toward the end of this chapter in the Humanities section.

Also consider fun, challenging activities such as chess clubs, engineering clubs, and homeschool academic teams that might be available in your area for the mathematically gifted. Even the use of video games can foster a strong practice of mathematical skills as a child must plan, make crucial decisions, and balance variables (Bossé & Rotigel, 2006). Universities, especially those that house gifted and talented programs, often offer summer camp-like environments focusing on gifted math (and science) topics.

Sometimes, there is still a stigma in the United States that girls are not quite as capable as boys in the areas of math and science. Your gifted daughter may need extra encouragement from you and others to recognize her true potential (Bossé & Rotigel, 2006). Surround her with biographies of historically notable women in her areas of interest. Look for opportunities for her to be around other mathematically and scientifically gifted females, both peers and otherwise. Tell her about careers in these fields and find ways to meet, or even shadow, ladies who are successful in the careers that most interest her. Science, Technology, Engineering and Mathematics (STEM) programs are available nationwide and work to promote these areas for girls and minorities. Contact a nearby university to find out if there are any STEM opportunities available to your child.

For Those Who Struggle

Math can be very abstract, especially for those whose learning style is not logical/mathematical. For this reason, many children need a math program that transitions from concrete to abstract lessons. This typically comes in the form of hands-on learning, even for older children.

real-life example

> To teach division with remainders to my children, we worked out division problems with some sort of manipulative like pretzels. I would say, "Here are 24 pretzels. Let's pretend that you need to share the pretzels among five people. How many would each person get if you give them a fair share, and would there be any leftovers?" My children placed the pretzels in five equal piles and a leftover pile. Through manipulation of the pretzels, they could see that all five children get four pretzels and there are four leftovers remaining.
>
> After several experiences with manipulatives, I would write the division equation out for them and solve the written problem myself as they manipulated the objects. In this way, I transferred the concrete part of division to the abstract concept. Soon after, I allowed them to write equations themselves as they manipulated the objects. When ready, we dropped the manipulatives and only wrote the equations. Doing this allowed my children to create a picture in their minds of the concepts of division and remainders. An otherwise abstract concept was now connected to real life, and therefore made sense to my children.

Some textbook companies are beginning to recognize the need for concrete learning and will offer manipulative packages to go along with their lessons. However, this most often happens at the younger levels, with manipulatives left behind as students get older. This is a shame, because even complex ideas such as algebra could be understood better through the use of concrete lessons. If your current curriculum doesn't offer hands-on lessons, you don't necessarily need to rush out to by something new. Simple at-home ideas can be found for almost any math concept by doing a quick Internet search. Type in key words such as "hands-on lessons multiplication" or "using manipulatives to teach fractions" to find ways to supplement particular lessons when your child struggles.

homeschool toolbox

Here are some of the more well-known hands-on math curriculum choices.

- *Math-U-See* by Steven Demme
- *RightStart Mathematics* by Dr. Joan A. Cotter
- *Miquon Math* by Key Curriculum Press
- *Family Math* (only supplemental) by Jean Ker Stenmark, Virginia Thompson, and Ruth Cossey

I also have written a math how-to book that could be encouraging for parents of both gifted and struggling math learners. It's called *Loving Living Math* (ourjourneywestward.com) and teaches you how to supplement textbook learning with such things as logic, problem solving, literature, manipulatives, games, projects, and more.

Science

characteristics of a gifted scientist

(Brandwein, 1995)

> - Shows an intense interest in science topics
> - Is able to reason and generalize information
> - Thinks critically and orderly
> - Is detail oriented
> - Is a very alert observer
> - Asks a lot of questions or wants to know "why"
> - Creatively finds solutions or sees alternative solutions
> - Enjoys research

For Those Who Excel

Science and math are very closely related, so many of the suggestions I have listed in the math section will work for gifted science education, too. Allow your child to join math/science related clubs. Also look for wonderful opportunities through museums, zoos, aquariums, theme parks, nature centers, and other businesses that will challenge and excite your budding scientist. Many of these places even offer in-depth learning camps during the summer. My scientifically gifted nephew had the opportunity to attend space camp at the U.S. Space and Rocket Center in Huntsville, AL several years ago. He was interested in the field of space science before going, but the experience only served to excite him more and spur him toward soaking in more and more information on the topic.

Children gifted in science may love the opportunity to take part in science fair competitions. Almost all fairs expect a child to participate in local, regional and/or state competitions before becoming eligible for national level competitions. The best place I've found to begin finding competitions in my area include local homeschool support groups who will pass along information regarding local level science fairs. The second best avenue I've found is to search for "science fair (insert state name)" on the Internet. This will lead you to one or more websites where state level competitions take place. On these websites, you will find affiliated local and regional competitions which your child might need to take part in before advancing to the state level. If you're interested in a particular national level competition, it's easiest to search their website and work your way through their chain of competitions to find the nearest local option.

homeschool toolbox

These are some of the national science fair competitions you might like to learn more about.

- Broadcom Masters Competition – student.societyforscience.org/broadcom-masters
- Intel International Science and Engineering Fair – student.societyforscience.org/intel-isef
- Junior Science and Humanities Symposium – jshs.org
- U.S. National BioGENEius Challenge – biotechinstitute.org

Because science concepts are rarely taught in incremental skills, worrying about skipping grade levels is usually not a problem. The biggest consideration you need to make is whether or not your child can handle the math necessary for upper level courses like biology, physics, and chemistry. If she's not ready for the required math, you'll be pleased to know that resources are almost endless for every science subject at intermediate levels. In other words, through curricula, experiment kits, library books, DVDs, programs, and more, your child can soak up all sorts of information before she's ready to dive into the courses that require complex math skills.

For your gifted scientist, my best advice is to let her take the lead in learning. You will, of course, need to make sure that all of the major disciplines are covered at some point including biology, Earth science, physics, and chemistry. She will be so thankful for the freedom to soar!

For Those Who Struggle

Most of the time, the issue isn't that a child can't understand science, but that she's disinterested. To solve this problem, make science interesting and fun. At least occasionally, let your child choose the science topic. If she's interested from the beginning, your job of making lessons fun will be much easier. Depending on her learning style, interject experiments, projects, graphic-filled books, DVDs, and games. You don't even really need a proper curriculum to create a thorough, fun study on a topic. Libraries house wonderful books full of information and built-in experiments that can serve as the main "text" of your study. When your child loses interest, move on to something else. The sciences often intermingle, so it's very likely the same topic will be covered again in a different study at some point.

Don't forget clubs and special classes for struggling scientists! These might be just the ticket to spark some enthusiasm. Also consider outdoor science in the form of gardening and nature walks. Both provide many opportunities for a wealth of scientific learning through a less typical approach. If you like the ideas of this approach, I have written NaturExplorers curriculum guides (ourjourneywestward.com) that encourage learning in all of the sciences through nature study. I've also found my local 4-H club to be a huge source of science related classes in the areas of agriculture, botany, horses, electricity, and more.

If you find that the content of a curriculum *is* actually too hard, you have a few choices. First, you can supplement or replace a particular lesson that's too difficult. For example, ask your child to read a book on the subject from the library in place of the chapter in the textbook. Or, search online for a different lesson on the same topic that you could use to help her understand it better.

Second, you might decide that the particular concept will be taught again at some point and skip over it entirely this time around. I did that with some of my daughter's physical science lessons that just didn't click when she was in seventh grade. I knew the same concepts would be covered again in physics a few years from that point, so I wasn't worried about complete mastery at the moment.

Third, you can step down to a simpler curriculum that teaches the same concepts. If your teen is really struggling with a high school chemistry text, there are chemistry texts available for middle school that will acceptably teach the concepts with less frustration. However, when deciding to do this, you will need to consider whether a particular course is a necessity for a transcript or not.

History/Social Studies

Characteristics of a Gifted Historian

(Johnsen, 2003)

> - Is intensely interested in history, social causes, politics, or cultures
> - Makes connections easily
> - Is able to understand relationships between things
> - Likes to argue "the other side" of an issue
> - Enjoys research and/or documentation
> - Loves listening to or retelling family stories or historical stories
> - Is reflective

For Those Who Excel

As with science, the sky is the limit for children who are deeply interested in history or social studies topics. Because of that reason, I will give similar advice. If there are opportunities in the form of clubs, special classes, courses, field trips, political internships, or otherwise that interest your child, let him take part. Contact museums, historical societies, historical sites, local governments, libraries, politicians, and local history buffs to find exciting options. Give him time to dive into books, DVDs, and projects on his subject of choice, too.

Your history student who also enjoys writing might like interviewing family members and creating a book of family history. Or, he might gather first person accounts of an event in history and write a book. If he isn't interested in writing, maybe a video documentary of the interviews would spark interest. Maybe he would prefer to interview nursing home residents about their favorite memories and write an article for the local newspaper. No matter the mode, encourage your historian to focus on primary sources for gathering information and to "do something" with all the wonderful information he learns.

Besides interviews, here are a few other close-to-home projects that might interest your history lover. Visit a cemetery and go on a history scavenger hunt (see Figure 1). Take a walking tour of your town where your child photographs important sites and then puts the photos together with research to create a photographic history. Visit various community offices – firehouse, police station, courthouse, post office, and so on – and learn how their services have changed over the years. Compile a book of timelines showing the progress of the community. Ideas like these are endless. Know what drives your child's passion and together, you and he can design wonderful learning opportunities.

Your history or geography buffs may also enjoy taking part in competitions. Although not quite as popular as science competitions, you might be surprised at the options available locally, regionally, and at the state level. As I mentioned when talking about science, my first avenue for learning about these competitions is through our local homeschool support group. However, searching online for "(insert state name) history competition" or "(insert state name) geography competition" will turn up results, too.

Figure 1. Cemetery Scavenger Hunt

Cemetery Scavenger Hunt

1. What is the oldest date you can find on a tombstone?
2. What is the newest date you can find on a tombstone?
3. How many people can you find who died during the time of the Civil War (April 12, 1861 – April 9, 1865)?
4. Can you tell if any of those deaths were a result of the war?
5. Look for tombstones of children. Do you find more deaths during one particular year or era than others? If so, consider researching if there was a plague or some form of destruction during that time period.
6. How many gravesites of veterans can you find? How do you know they are veterans?
7. What's the longest period of time you can find between the death of a husband and wife? Who died first?
8. Find a large family plot and try to make the familial connections by reading notes on the tombstones.
9. Find a large marker and note what other information you find on the marker besides the name and dates of the deceased.
10. Draw some of the symbols you find on various tombstones. Use the following website to research the meanings of each of the symbols. http://www.graveaddiction.com/symbol.html
11. Can you find any photographs on tombstones? What do the photos tell you about the person/era?
12. Choose a time period (like 1900-1940) and list the most common last names in the area during that time.
13. Is there a gravestone of anyone famous in the cemetery? Who is it and why were they famous?
14. Is there a different section of the cemetery dedicated to poor people or other groups? See if you can find out why there was a designation made.
15. An epitaph is a quote, phrase or statement written on a tombstone. Find one that is funny, sad, spiritual, and interesting. What can you learn about each person through their epitaph?
16. Find a tombstone that tells the job(s) someone held. What can you learn about the person from this information?
17. How many different materials can you find that have been used to make various tombstones? Does one era typically use one material versus another? Why?
18. Can you find a grave that dates before your state actually became a state?
19. Find one person who lived more than 80 years and make a simple timeline of major events he or she lived through.
20. Draw some of the various shapes of tombstones. Is one style more popular than the others? Why?

homeschool toolbox

A few national competitions you might consider include:

- The National History Bee – aceqb.com/historybee
- National History Day Contest – nhd.org/national-contest
- National Geographic Bee – nationalgeographic.org/bee

Personally, I learn history best when taught chronologically. I realize that not everyone needs that picture in their mind to organize and understand history, especially those who are naturally gifted in the subject. However, I have still insisted with my child gifted in history that he go through at least one 4-year cycle of history chronologically. The first year focuses on ancient history, the second on medieval history, the third on early modern history, and the fourth on late modern history. If your child balks at these limitations, you might consider having him keep a timeline (either in a notebook or on the wall) as he studies history on his own terms, so he can at least have a reference point as to how one era or person fits with another.

As with science, if you allow your child to go through these topics as they interest him, you will want to be sure that all major historical events, government systems, geography topics, and economics are taught at some point.

For Those Who Struggle

Again, it's quite likely that a child is simply not interested in history or social studies rather than not being able to grasp it. Unlike when we were in school, history and social studies don't have to be about reading boring textbooks and answering irrelevant quiz questions. For whatever time period or social studies topic you want to cover, make it fun. Read aloud or assign historical fiction to immerse your child into the time period. Take field trips, bake, do crafts, complete projects, watch DVDs, and read graphic-rich library books to make the subject matter come alive. As with science, your library will have activity books based on history topics that will supply you with all sorts of fun ideas and resources. Free preplanned unit studies can be found through a quick search on the Internet that will supply you with great ideas for any history or social studies topic. Simply search "free (insert history topic) unit study" or "ideas for teaching (insert history topic)."

If you find that your child understands particular historical events, but has a hard time connecting one event to another, or understanding where in history it takes place, consider creating a timeline or history notebook. Every time a new person or event is studied, your child can add a picture or phrase to his timeline. Or, he can create a simple page about the person or event and place it chronologically in a large three-ring binder. Over the years, the timeline or notebook will give a wonderful visual of where each thing fits as it relates to world history.

homeschool toolbox

If you are interested in studying history chronologically, I suggest the following:

> *Story of the World: History for the Classical Child* by Susan Wise Bauer
> *Beautiful Feet Books* by Rea Berg
> *The Mystery of History* by Linda Hobar.

Building a history wiki or website with your child is another way to pique interest. Wikis are easily edited, and many wiki sites are free to use (wikispaces.com). The benefit of this type of project is that when another child studies the same time period later, he or she can also add new information to the wiki.

Connections might be better made if your student picks a topic that interests him and then studies it throughout history. For example, a child interested in clothing and fashion design might look at the changes in dress in America throughout different time periods, from the modest clothing of the Shakers to seeing how pants became acceptable for women when they began to take on the jobs of men who were off fighting during World War II. This type of thematic study will allow students to see history chronologically and understand important events through the lens of something they are passionate about.

Fine Arts

characteristics of a child gifted in the arts

(Haroutounian, 1995)

> - A child gifted in drama may be dramatic herself, enjoy having an audience, like to reenact stories and events, often communicates with voice inflection and gestures, and can easily switch from one character to another when reading a story or acting out a scene.
> - A child gifted in music may need little or no instruction to sing or play an instrument well, has a good sense of rhythm, can hear pitches and harmonies easily, understands musical relationships, is typically well-coordinated, and expresses himself through or responds emotionally to music.
> - A child gifted in dance may be well-coordinated and physically balanced, have a good sense of rhythm and be able to remember sequences of choreography, enjoy music, express herself or respond emotionally to music, and be able to tell a story through dance.
> - A child gifted in art may be able to complete art projects with little or no instruction, evoke emotion from his artwork, find that he expresses himself easily through artwork, use creative ideas or media in his work, and enjoy viewing and critiquing artwork from other artists.

For Those Who Excel

Art, music, and drama are passions that define some gifted kids. Although some people might not consider these academically relevant, it would be hard to convince the gifted child of that fact! As the parent, you must recognize how important one or more of these is to your child and then do what you can to give him time and opportunities to develop his talents.

Search for lessons, groups, clubs, camps, field trips, and special classes for your child, according to your budget. There are many options available to homeschoolers.

Places to consider for fine arts training and opportunities include:

Drama

- Children's theater
- Community theater
- Historical reenactments
- Museums (often present skits as part of the museum experience, especially history museums)
- Puppetry clubs (see if any local churches host these)
- Co-ops and churches (often perform plays or have drama clubs)
- Weekend and summer camps at theaters and museums
- Individual or group drama classes

Music

- Private or group lessons for voice or an instrument
- Children's and community theaters (may offer singing or instrumental options)
- Community, youth, or church choirs or orchestras
- Colleges (often host summer traveling choirs or orchestras for high-school-aged students)
- Summer music camps sponsored by theaters, local teachers, schools, or colleges
- Fairs and other local venues often host talent competitions

Dance

- Private or group lessons
- Children's theaters and community theaters (will often have opportunities for ballets or other dance programming)
- Summer dance camps sponsored by theaters, local teachers, schools, or colleges
- Summer classes or weekend clinics hosted by college and high school dance troupes and cheerleading teams
- YMCA and other gym-sponsored programs or classes
- Fairs and other local venues often host talent competitions

Art

- Private or group lessons
- Local competitions or display opportunities sponsored by libraries, museums, 4-H clubs, colleges, or community projects
- Summer or weekend art camps hosted by art museums, schools, colleges, or local artists
- Festivals (especially ones that will have artists and craftspeople on hand to demonstrate and teach skills)
- Local theaters and museums (for tasks such as set production)
- Fashion shows

Besides formal training in the arts, most children devour observing others' work in their passion area. These children not only simply enjoy the genre, but also love seeing how others interpret emotions or use various techniques – quite a mode of instruction itself! Find many opportunities to visit art museums, operas, Broadway-style shows, and the like. Even viewing dances, dramas, or orchestras on television or the Internet can satisfy some children's desire to see more and learn more about the arts.

Also, remember how critically important it will be to practice skills at home. Not only should you allow for plenty of time, but also the necessary materials – instruments, dress-up clothes, art supplies, and so on. Oh, and when he wants to paint for hours and it drives you crazy, just grit your teeth and smile. When he wants to prepare productions for family and friends, support him.

Technology (more on this in the next chapter) has provided a fantastic outlet for budding artists of all types to showcase their talents. Blogs, which are often free and easy to use, offer a fantastic platform for "publishing" work. Photographs of artwork and videos of musical performances, dances, or dramas can all be posted on the Internet. Blog security can be set so that only certain people have access to your child's site, or your child could go public and potentially make a name for himself. If your child wants to sell artwork or handicrafts (e.g., knitting, woodworking), it's even possible to begin a small business on your own website. If you'd rather not go the route of creating a website, there is at least one art museum called Artsonia (artsonia.com/parents/) that will publish works of art for your child in an online gallery.

For Those Who Struggle

If your child doesn't excel in art, drama, dance, or music, don't worry. It's also okay if you'd like to expose him to the fine arts in hopes that he might find a new talent. Just be sure that you don't push too hard for a Mikhail Baryshnikov when he was made to be a Charlie Chapman.

Just as you would offer a gifted student lessons, groups, clubs, camps, field trips, and special classes, you can do so for a not-so-gifted child. If nothing else, the exposure to the fine arts will build an appreciation for later in his life.

Humanities

I have titled this section "humanities" for lack of a better word. There are some "extras" in which many gifted children excel that aren't necessarily their own subjects, but deserve more attention than just being included with one of the subjects listed previously. Because they are not must-teach courses in most instances, I've chosen not to talk about how to help children who struggle, but instead have only supplied ideas for encouraging the topics with your gifted or interested children.

Philosophy

Philosophy is the art of thinking, gaining knowledge, and developing conclusions. If your child is a deep thinker or is always asking questions, she may like some formal training in philosophy. In our home, we start teaching philosophy very young by considering the actions and behavior of characters from children's books. This is very easily done and doesn't require much teacher preparation at all. Using just about any book that you and your child read together, for instance *The Little Red Hen* by Paul Galdone, simply start asking open ended questions like, "Do you think the little red hen was right not to allow her friends to eat the bread?" "Why do you think she made that decision?" "How should her friends respond?" "What could the little red hen have done differently in the beginning of the book to help the situation?"

Through these discussions, my children begin contemplating issues and learning to draw conclusions. Of course, part of my motivation for this training is to teach my family's morals and values through the discussions, but I let my children do much of the thinking on their own before interjecting my own thoughts. If you're interested in the idea of encouraging philosophy through children's books, Teaching Children Philosophy (teachingchildrenphilosophy.org/BookModule/BookModule) maintains a fantastic website of book lists, topics, and questions for your child to ponder. If you'd like to tie some of these topics into the Bible, *For Instruction in Righteousness: A Topical Reference Guide for Biblical Child-Training* by Pam Forster is very thorough and helpful.

As my children get older, I try to encourage philosophical discussion frequently – about the books we read, television shows we watch, issues that arise around us, and especially apologetics.

homeschool toolbox

Besides simple philosophical discussions around the house, there are more formal methods of teaching philosophy which can be used at home or with groups of children for livelier lessons.

- *The Examined Life: Advanced Philosophy for Kids* by David White, PhD
- *More Philosophy for Teens: Examining Reality and Knowledge* by Paul Thomson, PhD and Sharon Kaye, PhD
- *Philosophy for Kids: 40 Fun Questions that Help You Wonder About Everything!* by David White, PhD
- *Philosophy for Teens: Examining Life's Big Ideas* by Sharon Kaye, PhD and Paul Thomson, PhD
- *Really, Really Big Questions About Life, the Universe, and Everything* by Stephen Law

Debate

Debate is very closely tied to philosophy by the fact that one must determine his beliefs about a topic before defending those beliefs in a formal discussion. Children who like philosophy, public speaking, and/or arguing or defending themselves are good candidates for learning the art of debate. Whereas philosophy can be practiced alone or in groups, debate requires more than one person so that varied sides of an issue can be discussed. You don't have to take part in a formal debate club to learn how to debate, but clubs can offer lively (and cooperative) sessions that kids who enjoy debate often prefer. You can often find homeschool debate clubs locally, but if not, start your own through the National Christian Forensic and Communications Association (ncfca.org).

homeschool toolbox

Although most of these are written for group situations, the ideas in the following books can be easily altered for use with only two or three people.

- *Jeub's Complete Guide to Speech and Debate* by Chris Jeub.
- *Make Up Your Mind: A Classroom Guide to 10 Age-Old Debates* by Clark Porter, PhD and James Girsch, PhD
- *What's Your Opinion?: An Interactive Discovery-Based Language Arts Unit for High Ability Learners* by Richard Cote and Darcy Blauvelt.

Public Speaking

If your child enjoys public speaking, but not necessarily debate, consider speech clubs instead. Most local 4-H extension programs offer speech clubs and competitions which welcome homeschoolers. Many homeschool co-ops will also offer public speaking courses and platforms.

homeschool toolbox

The following national and international organizations offer wonderful speaking, speech, and/or debate opportunities and competitions.

- Institute for Cultural Communicators – iccinc.org
- National Christian Forensic and Communications Association – ncfca.org
- National Forensic League – speechanddebate.org
- Toastmasters International – toastmasters.org

Leadership

Some children thrive in leadership roles of all types. Because these roles are available nearly everywhere you look *and* will depend greatly on a child's interests, I can't possibly give you an exhaustive list of places to look for leadership opportunities. However, I'll offer a small list of places you might consider when thinking about where your child can practice being the leader she was made to be.

- Many clubs offer leadership offices. Think about clubs like 4-H, Future Farmers of America, Boy Scouts and Girl Scouts, public school clubs (if your homeschoolers are allowed to take part), and even more adult-minded civic clubs like Civitan International or Kiwanis International.
- Your child can organize a club, field trip, service outing, or ministry of his or her own choosing.
- Have your child teach a class. Anything goes from Vacation Bible School, to musical instruments, to tutoring services.
- Your child can serve on youth council boards. We live near the Kentucky Horse Park, where the Kentucky Equine Education Project is housed, that offers a youth council board on which my daughter was able to serve. It combined her love of horses with her passion for leadership seamlessly.
- Your child could serve as captain of a sports team or academic team.
- TeenPact (teenpact.com) offers political leadership opportunities, or you might consider volunteering your family to work on a political campaign.
- Your child can volunteer to help with anything from the soup kitchen to community event planning.
- Have your child attend (or even help with) leadership conferences. Two of my children have had the opportunity to attend a youth leadership conference at a nearby Christian college and have

volunteered to help with various tasks for our state's homeschooling convention.

Logic

Logic is one of my favorite "additions" to our homeschool. When I use the term logic, I'm actually referring to two different (both important) facets. The first is what I'll call "mathematical/scientific logic," and the second I'll call "formal logic." Although many people would argue that children aren't ready for either facet until the upper grades, I firmly believe that logical thinking can begin as early as preschool. I certainly don't mean that preschoolers are able to reason like adults, but I do mean that training the mind to think logically can begin very early. For gifted children who are far ahead in making logical connections, all the more reason to further this skill.

Mathematical/scientific logic includes such things as patterns, analogies, if-then statements, truth statements, and inferences based on clues. One of our favorite forms of mathematical/scientific logic is in completing logic matrix puzzles.

This facet of logic is easy to start with young children, and just as easy to continue all the way through high school. For little ones, pull out math manipulatives and make patterns, sort a pile of various objects based on classification attributes (all the round things go here, all the things with sides go there), or play I-Spy games based on clues that build upon one another. There are plenty of games and resource books available, even for preschoolers, to encourage this sort of thinking.

homeschool toolbox

The following lists provide logic resources for use with children in pre-school-grade 2:

Games	Books
Animalogic	*Lollipop Logic* and *Lollipop Logic 2* by Bonnie Risby and Robert Risby
Connect Four	
Guess Who?	*Primarily Bears* by Maurine Allen
Logic Links	
Meta Forms	
Zoologic	

For children from second grade through high school, there are a wealth of wonderful mathematical/scientific logic activities to do. From the very beginning of our homeschooling journey, we have included at least one "logic day" per week and my children literally beg for that day to arrive. They aren't the only ones who have grown to love this method of critical thinking; I enjoy the time as much as them. If you have a child who is very logically/mathematically gifted, he is sure to enjoy any logic you send his way. However, because I've seen such fruition in all aspects of my children's lives by training them to think logically, I highly recommend adding logic days whether your child has a logical/mathematical talent or not.

homeschool toolbox

Because so many of the resources below are either appropriate for a very large age range, or include a series of books available for all age levels, here is a large list of my favorite logic resources appropriate for grades 2-12.

Games	Books
10 Days in...games	*Logic Countdown* and *Logic Liftoff* by Bonnie Risby
Battleship	
Blokus	*Logic Posters, Problems and Puzzles* by Honi Bamberger
Checkers	
Chess	*Logic Safari* by Bonnie Risby
Clue	*Mind Benders* by Critical Thinking Press
Knot So Fast	
Mancala	*One Hour Mysteries* and *More One Hour Mysteries* by Mary Ann Carr
Mastermind	
Noodlers	*The Great Chocolate Caper* by Mary Ann Carr
Qwirkle	
Risk	
River Crossing	
Rush Hour	
Sequence	
SET	

Formal logic is just as the name suggests – a more formal study of logic and reason. Although it's true that you can train your children to begin thinking logically at an early age, logical reasoning is usually saved for the older gifted child who is able to understand and apply the principles of reasoning. These principles include such things as deductions, abductions, and inductions; recognizing and naming propaganda; understanding and recognizing fallacies in arguments: and much more. The ability to think abstractly is a must when teaching formal logic. Most children transition from concrete thinking to abstract thinking around the age of 12; however, some gifted children transition much earlier. This facet of logic will allow your child to think clearly and critically for a lifetime.

homeschool toolbox

We have used (and loved) each of the reasoning logic resources below.

- *Art of the Argument: An Introduction to the Informal Fallacies* by Aaron Lawson and Joelle Hodge
- *The Discovery of Deduction: An Introduction to Informal Logic* by Aaron Lawson, Joelle Hodge, and Shelly Johnson
- *The Thinking Toolbox* and *The Fallacy Detective* by Nathaniel Bluedorn and Hans Bluedorn
- *Traditional Logic* and *Material Logic* by Martin Cothran

I hope this chapter has not only given you an abundance of ideas for meeting the needs of your gifted and twice-exceptional children, but serves to ignite your creativity as you design your own fantastic ideas!

chapter 5

Technology and the Gifted Homeschooler

Laptops and iPhones and apps, oh my! Our kids are part of a giant technological boom, whether we like it or not, or whether we as parents understand it or not. It's of utmost importance that our children become technologically savvy and it's our job as homeschooling parents to see that they do. For this reason, I'm including an entire chapter on the subject of how to effectively incorporate technology into your homeschool.

Not too many years ago, one argument against homeschooling was that schools, unlike homes, had all the newest technology available, along with teachers who actually understood it. Luckily, the latest technologies aren't out of reach for families anymore, so homeschoolers have just as many (if not more) opportunities for working with technology and becoming experts. Also, luckily, our children seem to naturally grasp onto technological know-how without a great deal of instruction. As the parent, you will want to be sure your child has an understanding of certain technologies, whether he figures it out on his own, you teach him, or you find another teacher or curriculum.

Realizing that technology is ever-changing, if I were to list the very basic technology a child ought to master before graduating homeschool, it would include:

- general computer/laptop/tablet knowledge;
- using basic operating systems (Windows, Mac OS);
- general Internet research and use;
- online safety;
- typing skills;
- word processing skills and use of word processing programs;
- use of spreadsheet programs;
- creation of slideshows and presentations;
- basic photo editing;
- connecting devices and transferring files;
- downloading and uploading files;
- using external devices such as smart phones, tablets, digital cameras, iPods, webcams, and so on; and
- using televisions, DVD players, and console games and knowing how to interconnect them.

Additionally, children who are technologically gifted or have an interest in the fields of graphic design, engineering, architecture, drafting, computer technology, website development, computer programming, photography, or the media may want to dabble in the following:

- HTML, Java, C++, and other computer languages;
- website design;
- computer networking;
- computer programming;
- computer repair;
- film production/editing;
- music production/editing;
- advanced photo editing; and
- graphic design programs like Adobe Photoshop and Adobe InDesign.

With All of the Possibilities, Where's a Parent to Start?

No matter the age or giftedness of the student, you will want to start with the basics and develop skills and experiences as he's ready. Don't worry if you don't own all the latest technologies. If you have a desktop computer or laptop with Internet connection, you'll be able to cover much of the basic technology list. Additionally, once your child masters one other device, such as a cell phone or game console, he will easily catch on to other similar devices.

homeschool toolbox

But what if you haven't a clue what some of these techy things are, much less how to teach them? You'll be glad to know that there are at least three companies who write curriculum specifically geared toward teaching homeschoolers about computers and other technologies.

- Computer Science for Kids – computerscienceforkids.com
- CompuScholar – compuscholar.com
- Motherboard Books – motherboardbooks.com

What if purchasing a computer curriculum still sends shivers of fear up and down your spine? Find a teacher or two to help out. Community education programs and local libraries often host very inexpensive computer classes open for all ages. Many times, homeschool co-ops will host computer classes, too. If your child is old enough based on a community college's regulations, he could take a wide variety of computer classes for a fee. As with just about any other subject, computer classes can be taken online, too, through various distance learning sources. You will find a wealth of distance learning options by typing "online computer classes" into your Internet browser. Also, don't discount a friendly tech-savvy teenager who might be willing to tutor your child on some of the more elusive topics.

homeschool hint

All suggestions relating to the Internet assume that you will be supervising your child. Be sure to read the section at the end of the chapter for very important online safety tips.

Integrating Technology into Your Homeschool

Besides teaching specific computer classes, there are wonderful ways to incorporate the use of technology into everyday lessons. The only limit is your imagination! I'll supply you with several ideas that I hope will get your creative juices flowing.

- For general computer know-how, I have used Click-N-Learn: What's Inside a Computer? (kids-online.net/learn/c_n_l.html) to help my children understand the parts and functions of the computer.
- I have also allowed my children to disassemble old electronic products in order to get to know various pieces and parts and how they work together.
- Find a fun typing program that only takes a few minutes a day and will encourage proper hand placement and speed. Dance Mat Typing (kidztype.com) and Type Dojo (typedojo.com) are two free websites I have used and my children have enjoyed. You can also purchase more

in-depth and flashy programs such as Typing Instructor by Individual Software and Mavis Beacon Teaches Typing by Encore Software.
- For Internet surfing practice, send your child on an Internet scavenger hunt. Use the ideas provided in Figure 2 or make up a hunt of your own.

Internet Scavenger Hunt

Follow the directions to find various things on the Internet. Note your findings beside each task.

1. Find a book from your local library on the topic of the American Revolution. Write the title and author of the book.

2. On Amazon.com, find a product for gardening. What is the product and how much does it cost?

3. Find the weather page of your local news station and write the current temperature.

4. Type your address into maps.google.com. Is the map accurate?

5. Locate and write the telephone number of your county sheriff's office.

6. Find the website for an historical site in your area. What are the hours of operation?

7. What is the title of an upcoming movie at your nearest movie theater?

8. What is the difference between the cost of an adult ticket and child's ticket for a nearby museum?

9. What are two of the attractions at the nearest zoo?

10. What are optimal growing conditions for boxwood shrubs?

Figure 2. Internet Scavenger Hunt

- Another activity to encourage Internet practice is asking your child to write a research paper using only Internet resources. Allow her to insert images into a word processing document in which she's typed her final draft. Make sure she includes credits for the images she uses (this is a great way to teach kids about plagiarism and properly giving credit to others' work).
- Other fun sources for integrating Internet surfing into school work are *Problem-Based Learning With the Internet* by William Stepien for grades 3–6 and *The Internet and Problem-Based Learning* by William J. Stepien, William C. Stepien and Peter Senn for grades 6–12.
- Allow your child to use a newsletter template in your word processing program to create a homeschool happenings newsletter to send to family members. Include photos, original stories, short articles about classes they've been taking, and other news. See a sample newsletter in Figure 3.

Figure 3

- If your child starts a business like a lemonade stand or lawn care company, he can create posters and business cards in a word processing program, too.
- Let her use a slide show program, such as PowerPoint, to create a research project. In other words, instead of writing a typical research paper to go along with a history assignment or science fair project, she can compile the research and photos into a slideshow presentation. Music can be integrated for extra effect.
- Your child can use a spreadsheet program, like Excel, to create computerized graphs after surveying family and friends on a topic. For example, after asking 25 people about their favorite book genre, he could create a full-color bar graph of the results using the spreadsheet program. Figure 4 shows another option for graph creation. Create-A-Graph (nces.ed.gov/nceskids/createagraph/) is a free online graphing tool that is even easier to use than a regular spreadsheet program. In this particular example, my son designed and tested various paper airplane styles and then assimilated the information in a unique 3-D bar graph.

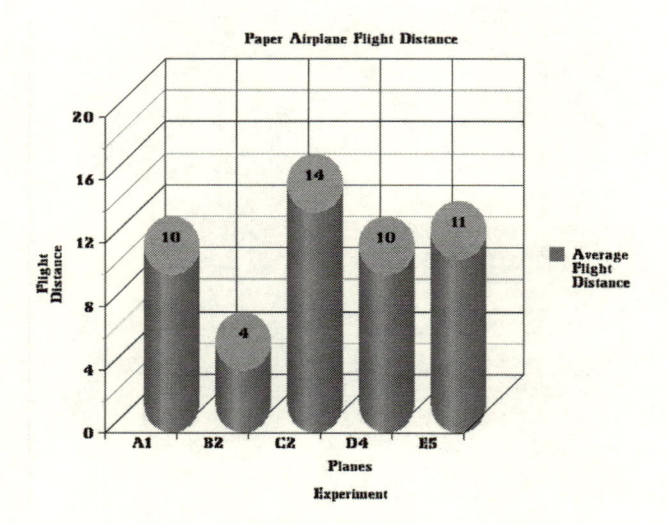

Figure 4

- Ask your child to plan her birthday party from start to finish using a program like OneNote to keep detailed notes.
- Blogging is a fantastic outlet for a child who loves to write or loves to fiddle with website design. It's also a motivator for a child who hates to write. Something about seeing a "published" draft so quickly inspires reluctant writers.
- Social media sites like Facebook, Instagram, or Snapchat – with very careful monitoring – are another great way to encourage good writing and typing skills for older kids.
- Partner with another family or a small group of families and ask the children to write a collaborative story using a service like Google Docs (docs.google.com) or Dropbox (dropbox.com) where each person can be granted access to the material. One person can start the story and "pass it on" to the next person very easily.
- After writing a story, encourage your child to use a site like Blurb (blurb.com) to create a real published book. Your child will be able to upload her text and add photos or images, designing her pages how she sees fit. When she's finished, she gets to choose a book style and, for a fee, it will be printed and sent to your home. These make fantastic keepsakes, as well as gifts.
- Let him use a basic photo editing program (they often come with newer computers) to edit 10 photos. Print the photos and use them as the graphics in a comic book he writes.
- Use a program like Windows Movie Maker or iMovie (which may have come with your computer) to create a commercial, newscast, or other fun project. She will be able to add images, video, sound effects, sound tracks, and voice-overs, making the possibilities endless.
- Ask your child to use a map site like Google Maps (map.google.com) to chart the course for an upcoming field trip or vacation.
- Your child can find, download, and listen to a podcast class on a subject relevant to what he is learning.
- If your child has a pen pal, encourage the (safe!) use of e-mail and/or webcam meetings.

- If you own a GPS-capable device, use it to go geocaching for a fun-filled family geography hike. Geocaching.com will explain the concept and help you find maps in your area.

Although probably obvious, computer software, gaming systems, and wireless devices all have an incredible number of academically strong games that can challenge or remediate in fun ways. I couldn't possibly list all of the sources for learning games and apps since they are available for almost every computerized device on the market from hundreds of sources. However, a quick online search of your needs should turn up a wealth of possibilities. For instance, if your first grader needs phonics help and you own both a computer and iPhone, you could type in "phonics software first grade" on your computer browser or "phonics" into your phone's app store to find and compare several choices.

homeschool hint

When you or your child is struggling with something related to school, there is probably at least one website tutorial and/or YouTube video to clear up the confusion. Again, a quick online search will lead to several options. Also, video clips are widely available to teach about historical events, demonstrate science experiments, and many other things of educational value.

There are several technological options for engaging your child academically when running errands, sitting in a waiting room, or shuttling to a class across town, too. In the car, listen to audiobooks that the entire family can enjoy together. Consider downloading several eBooks onto one of your devices that can be read in the car or a waiting room. Additionally, educational apps or learning games for gaming systems like the Nintendo DS are great for keeping busy hands and minds occupied.

Technology is also available in the form of complete curriculum. Some curriculum companies such as Switched-On Schoolhouse by Alpha Omega

Publishing are entirely computer-based. Children read their lessons on the computer and complete most of the work on the computer as well. Besides appealing to some children simply for the non-traditional schooling aspect, the lessons are often interactive and have immediate, built-in review if answers are incorrect. If the idea of some computerized classes sounds good, but you wouldn't want to complete the entire curriculum in this manner, various courses can be purchased separately.

Additionally, many companies are offering virtual teachers and step-by-step answer keys via the computer. As my children enter the higher levels of math, for example, they watch a virtual teacher on a CD-ROM present each day's lesson before they attempt the problem set. If they stumble upon a sticky problem, the program will work through the problem one step at a time. This is immensely helpful for both my children and me. Since curriculum choices are so varied and there are so many computerized helps available for various curricula, I will simply encourage you to check to see if your curriculum choices have computerized options by visiting the publisher's website.

Some curriculum choices are strictly internet-based. Time4Learning (time4learning.com), for instance, has developed a fee-based, multimedia homeschool curriculum for preschool through high school. They provide online lesson plans and a question and answer forum for the parents, too.

homeschool toolbox

Various universities offer computer-based courses specifically for gifted and talented students. While the list below is by no means exhaustive, some of the university programs offering these courses include:

- John Hopkins Center for Talented Youth – cty.jhu.edu/ctyonline/index.html
- Northwestern's Center for Talent Development – ctd.northwestern.edu/program_type/online-programs
- University of Connecticut's Gifted and Talented Online – gifted.education.uconn.edu/register-for-an-online-course

As with any internet-based course, including distance-learning classes from a community college or otherwise, high speed internet access is a must. The webpages are often full of graphics, videos, and interactives which will not work well on a slow connection.

As you can see, the homeschooled child is not lacking in technological opportunities! And, for the gifted child, there is no limit to how far he can soar through the use of technology. Whether he's technologically gifted or just uses technology as part of his other ventures, the world is his to seize with the help of computers and other exciting devices.

Online Safety

Our children can be online in a matter of seconds. Although tremendously helpful in most situations, the Internet can also be very dangerous, especially in the hands of a child or teen who doesn't understand the serious dangers. First, and foremost, online predators are happy to find our children. Then, you have the threat of identity theft, computer-damaging viruses, and inappropriate webpages. Homeschoolers not only integrate technology into schoolwork quite often, they might also have extra downtime in which technology could fill the time. Figure 5 includes a list of some precautions that I hope you'll find helpful in establishing safe Internet safety in your homeschool.

Internet Safety Tips

- ✓ Be with or nearby your child as often as possible when he is on the Internet.
- ✓ Add child-friendly safety filters. McAfee Safe Family (family.mcafee.com) and Covenant Eyes (covenanteyes.com) are two popular choices. Most mobile devices have built-in safety controls that can be easily set by the parent.
- ✓ Train your child in safe surfing practices such as using a site like CyberSlueth-Kids (cybersleuth-kids.com) as a search engine.
- ✓ Keep all Internet-linked computers and devices in public places in the house.
- ✓ Your child should know to never give his real name, address, phone number, Social Security number, or other personal information on the Internet – ever.
- ✓ Set family rules about chat sites.
- ✓ Parents should always know where a child goes online and his passwords. Communicate that it's a privilege to be allowed on the Internet, not a right.
- ✓ Check browsing histories and chat rooms often.
- ✓ Teach your child that he should never download files without permission.
- ✓ Teach him never to open an email from an unknown source.
- ✓ Encourage your child to talk with you when something questionable happens online so you can work through it together.

Figure 5: Internet Safety Tips

chapter 6

Individualizing Instruction

Teachers in public or private schools have to work hard to individualize instruction for all their varied learners. Typically, they term this method *differentiation*, meaning some children are expected or allowed to do something different than most of the rest of the class. Through differentiation, the students are closer to having their individual abilities stretched than if they were simply doing the same thing as everyone else in the class. Differentiation goes all ways – it's used for the gifted student and learning disabled student in inclusive classrooms as well as the average student. Luckily, homeschooling parents tend to meet each child's individual needs naturally, leaving less need for differentiation. However, if you are homeschooling more than one child, or still struggle with the idea of how to modify curriculum choices, this chapter will offer you some creative ideas for individualizing instruction.

Differentiation When Homeschooling More Than One Child

Parents often ask, "Only one of my children is gifted. How do I meet his needs and everyone else's at the same time?" There are several ways to go about meeting everyone's needs. First, and probably easiest to implement, is simply teaching each child his own lessons on his own levels. As easy as it sounds, this is *not* the most time effective for the parent. You will find yourself jumping from one child to the other and getting dizzy in between.

The next simplest option if you have independent learners is to assign appropriate work to each child and let them go off to complete it, only coming to you when questions arise. Although I'm a huge fan of training children to work independently, this pretty little picture isn't always reality. It won't fail that more often than not several children will need you for different purposes at the same time leading to more dizziness.

While there will be times during the day when your children will certainly need to complete work on their own level and you will get a bit dizzy in the process of meeting everyone's needs, there is another option. In many homeschools the parent will teach some subjects at the same time to all the children. For instance, everyone in the house may learn about the topic of rocks and minerals together. The parent might read a book on the topic with all the children and then embark on a nature walk where everyone finds samples to bring home. Upon returning home, the self-directed, gifted child may be asked to catalog all the finds using various identification tests and a field guide, while the other children complete a much simpler classification process with the parent. In this way, the learning is differentiated upon returning home – the gifted child is asked to "go for it" on her own with some in-depth classification, while the rest of the family takes a slower, more parent-directed path. Combining learning in this way can really take some of the pressure of buzzing from one child to the next off of you. Toward the end of the chapter, I will discuss project-based learning, which should help further explain some of the things you can offer your child for differentiation activities.

The subjects most easily taught to all students at the same time are science, history, social studies, and Bible lessons. Depending on the age span of your children, other subjects may lend themselves to group learning, too. For instance, if your children are 8 and 9 years old, it might not make much of a difference to work on the same spelling lists or grammar skills.

homeschool toolbox

Although written for public school teachers, there are some books available to help you learn some differentiation techniques.

- *Differentiated Instruction: Making it Work* by Patti Drapeau
- *Differentiating Instruction with Menus* series by Laurie E. Westphal
- *Differentiation Made Simple: Timesaving Tools for Teachers* by Mary Ann Carr
- *Differentiation That Really Works: Strategies from Real Teachers for Real Classrooms* by Cheryl M. Adams and Rebecca L. Pierce
- *Ready-to-Use Differentiation Strategies* by Laurie E. Westphal

Even with individualizing instruction, one of the hardest parts of teaching more than one child at once will be keeping your gifted child purposefully occupied, especially if he's active or not a self-starter. Be one step ahead of him. I like to set up creative centers around the house so there's always something challenging and interesting to do when schoolwork is finished. These areas, which can be set up all over the house (e.g., a coffee table, a shelf, a basket in the corner of the room), might include:

- a game;
- a few library books;
- a craft kit;
- art supplies;
- blank maps and an atlas;

- puzzles;
- a building kit;
- a creative toy like LEGO blocks;
- science experiment kits or books with supplies;
- logic puzzle; or
- yarn, knitting needles, and a knitting how-to book.

Insect Learning Center

real-life example

Center ideas are endless and can be implemented to further a learning passion or help your child consider something new without any pressure.

Passion: When my daughter passionately wanted to continue learning about WWI and the rest of us were ready to move on to another history topic, I created a center full of additional independent learning for her. It included a few non-fiction and historical fiction selections from the library; some blank maps, colored pencils and a book about where various battles took place; a book of artwork/propaganda from the era and art supplies; and a cookbook of recipes from the era. (As she grew older, I didn't have to provide as many centers because she had learned how to develop her own creative ideas for extending studies to meet her needs.)

Reluctance: My daughter wasn't passionate about every subject! Some science topics like insects and the human body were gross to her. When she was younger and preferred not to do an entire, lab-type study on insects, I opted for a fun summer center that was interesting enough to draw her attention, but low-key enough to keep her attention. I included a really good book about insects from the library; an insect field guide and a blank notebook in case she wanted to note any observations; some plastic insects and play dough for creating anatomically correct models without the need to touch or look at real bugs; and a bug collection box with a book of bug activities. I pulled several insect books from our home library shelves, and even found some bug stickers and flashcards at the dollar store to add to the center. I hoped she might be inspired to get over her icky thoughts about insects, but whether she did or not, she learned a lot about bugs in the end.

My children are free to work on a center whenever they like. I change out the contents often to keep the excitement stirred. I would also encourage you to keep creative supplies handy and allow your kids access to them whenever they like. These would include art and craft supplies, building materials, science experiment items, and so on. Be sure to keep a bookshelf of how-to books on all kinds of subjects to spark ideas for using all the wonderful supplies you've made available.

What If My Kids Say They're Bored?

Speaking of books, we have bookshelves full of great reading material—everything from magazines, to picture books, to chapter books, to audio books. Diving into a good book leaves little time for boredom.

Sports supplies, gardening supplies, scrap building materials and tools, kites, riding toys, other outdoor toys, and free spaces in the yard to build forts or grow gardens should also be made freely available to your children. Your active or creative child will thrive in the outdoor "classroom".

> **homeschool hint**
>
> Going outside for regular lessons can be a huge motivator for those ho-hum or frustrating days, too. Sit on a porch swing, lie on the trampoline, or spread out on a blanket under a shade tree, and watch the life of a typical lesson perk up.

Even with all these occupiers, you might still find a bored child. Consider creating a "100 Things To Do If I'm Bored" list. (See Figure 6 for a sample list I've given my children.) It can include everything from fun learning opportunities to chores around the house. I like to give my children additional motivation to use the list when they find they are bored. To make it fun for all, I allow them to highlight the to-dos as they are accomplished. After completing 10 of the items without complaint or prodding, a prize of some sort (like a trip to the ice cream store) is in order. After the entire list of 100 tasks is completed, a bigger family fun event (like a trip to the drive-in theater) takes place.

100 Things To Do If I'm Bored

1. read
2. ride a bike
3. take a nature walk
4. do an experiment
5. play an instrument
6. draw
7. play a board game
8. clean your room
9. wash windows
10. do a craft
11. play a card game
12. organize a book shelf
13. make a recipe
14. practice flashcards
15. call a friend
16. write a letter
17. play dress up
18. do a puzzle
19. make a mask
20. listen to music
21. weed the flowers
22. water the flowers
23. make up a story
24. act out a story
25. make up a song
26. listen to a book on tape
27. exercise
28. bird watch
29. do leaf rubbings
30. graph the number of bugs you see in an hour
31. collect seeds
32. actually play with your toys
33. do origami
34. create a science lesson to teach to a younger child
35. play a computer game
36. organize the refrigerator
37. read a magazine
38. dig in the garden
39. look up a word you don't know in the dictionary and try to use it throughout the day
40. collect rocks
41. paint rocks
42. write a Christmas wish list
43. make bubbles
44. jump rope
45. play in water
46. mop a bathroom
47. organize a drawer in your room
48. paint a picture
49. dance
50. watch the clouds go by
51. design your own science experiment
52. decorate a writing journal
53. teach your dogs a trick
54. experiment with new hairstyles
55. make some beaded jewelry
56. sew
57. knit
58. crochet
59. take a treat to a neighbor
60. wash the car
61. build something from wood scraps
62. plant seeds
63. practice a play to put on for your parents
64. skip
65. do jumping jacks
66. wash dishes
67. play hide and go seek
68. build with Lego blocks
69. play cowboys and Indians
70. pull out your spy journals
71. sort shells
72. play with pattern blocks
73. set up a picture studio
74. make play dough
75. make a healthy snack
76. plan a party
77. write a grocery list for Mom
78. memorize a poem and tell it to someone
79. play school
80. design an outfit
81. set up a store for your family to shop
82. help an elderly neighbor with a job around their house
83. make an instrument
84. take a nap
85. take a long bubble bath
86. vacuum the van
87. make clay boats to sail
88. make your own 100 things to do list
89. do a crossword puzzle
90. write and illustrate a story
91. study an artist and try one of his or her pieces
92. make silly faces in the mirror
93. swing
94. jump on the trampoline
95. make puppets
96. organize pictures
97. go through toys and choose some to give away
98. go through clothes and bag up the ones that are too small
99. make cards for you family or friends
100. draw the clouds in the sky

Figure 6: 100 Things To Do If I'm Bored

Also, remember that some children who are bored simply need more challenging work or assignments that fit their learning styles. The bottom line is that you will have to be prepared to combat the active, easily bored, or unmotivated child. All homeschool parents do. In fact, all parents do! If you come up with a plan and communicate it to your child early, it will save you many moments of chaos resulting from boredom.

In Making Sure I'm Meeting My Child's Needs, How Much Time Do I Devote to the Gifted Areas Versus the Other Areas?

One of the really cool parts about homeschooling is that everything tends to work together through various lessons and projects. So, if your child is a brilliant mathematician, you can assign projects that challenge her in math, while also including other subjects like reading, writing, and technology at the same time. The main thrust of the lesson will be the challenging math, but you won't be leaving out the other subjects either.

real-life example

When my math-advanced second grader needed some math challenges, but would not have been happy with more math worksheets, I had to think creatively. Because the Thanksgiving holiday was near, I asked him to send an email to his friends and family surveying them about their favorite Thanksgiving pie. As the emails came back in, he compiled the information on a tally chart, and then turned the information into a simple bar graph. Together, we transferred the information from the hand-drawn bar graph into a computerized spreadsheet bar graph so he could attach and forward the results of the survey to the friends and family who took part.

Throughout this one extension activity, he covered mathematics (tallying, graphing), computer skills (emailing, typing, spreadsheets, attachments), writing skills (writing the emails), and art skills (drawing the original graph). And, he was enthusiastic during each and every aspect. Had I assigned each of these subjects separately, rest assured that he would not have been such a happy camper. So, integrating the less-loved subjects with an activity in the strong subject made for a challenging, yet fun assignment.

When it comes to nurturing the gifted areas, I tend to have my children take care of their "busy" work early in the day, so they have time to pour themselves into their passion work later. However, if your child doesn't have a passion for her areas of strength, you can encourage higher level learning by assigning challenging work during the regular lesson time. For example, if she is gifted in math, but doesn't passionately devour it, you can simply work in a higher level book during regular math time. You can also make sure to include lots of challenging math games during a weekly family game night or encourage her to take part in a fun math quiz club via the local homeschooling group. In these less obvious ways you are encouraging growth and your child may never be the wiser.

Project-Based Learning

Project-based learning is a tool I use consistently in my homeschool for several reasons, the most important being the fact that it lends itself well to meeting individual needs while allowing me to teach more than one child the same topic. Additionally, asking your child to complete a project during or after his learning gives him a landing place without restrictions. Many gifted children want to jump into a subject feet first, but never have an ultimate plan or goal to do anything with the information. Assigning a final project gives all that depth and breadth of learning a place to come together. It gives him some accountability in learning, while offering an amazing scope of choices and open boundaries at the same time.

For the same reasons, project-based learning is a fantastic tool for unmotivated children, too. It offers choices in learning, choices in assignments, and a definite end in sight. Of my three children, one is self-motivated and the other two are mostly mom-motivated. Project-based learning brings out the best in all of them.

Just what is project-based learning? Quite simply, it's a learning method in which your child dives into a subject and completes some sort of project(s) to show what he knows. Projects can be anything under the sun.

Table 6. Projects List

Art	Article	Banner	Blog Post	Book Report
Brochure	Commercial	Construction	Cooking	Craft
Debate	Demonstration	Diagram	Diorama	Experiment
Fund-raiser	Graph	Handicraft	Instrumental	Journal
Magazine Layout	Map	Mobile	Model	Monologue
Movie	Mural	Newscast	Newsletter	Organizational Planner
Photogrpahy Exhibit	Play	Poem	Postcard	Poster
Power Point Presentation	Puppet Show	Puzzle	Report	Sales Pitch
Scrapbook	Skit	Song	Speech	Story
Storytelling	Timeline	Web Page	Website	Written Review

The project list I've included in Table 6 is by no means exhaustive. Use your child's interests and the resources available to you to write a list of potential project ideas to keep handy. Depending on your child's learning styles and desires, he can probably design some fantastic project ideas himself! When the time comes to create a project, having a list of possibilities already prepared will be helpful for both you and your child. A good book that includes tons of project ideas, especially for gifted students, and rubrics for evaluating each type of project is *The Ultimate Guide to Student Product Development and Evaluation* (2nd. Ed.) by Frances A. Karnes and Kristen R. Stephens.

Not only do projects allow me to individualize instruction easily, they also have helped my children understand and retain information greatly – as compared to simply learning about a topic and regurgitating the info back to me on a test. Why? Because children become part of the learning through their projects! In order to complete a project, they have to "know their stuff" about the topic *and* put it together in an organized, thoughtful, expressive way. I also expect my children to present their projects to the family to further embed the learning and to become comfortable with verbalizing themselves. Believe me, just because they can put together a super project, doesn't mean they can automatically speak about it. This is a separate skill to be learned, but just as important.

homeschool hint

Projects are so much more than simply wrapping up a time of learning in order to give a presentation. They also:

- encourage independent learning;
- require creative and critical thinking;
- require higher order thinking;
- require writing and research;
- tend to reach into many academic areas;
- allow choices to be made by the student;
- allow for meaningful, hands-on experiences;
- allow for varied learning styles to be met; and
- encourage real learning about a subject.

Project-based learning can be interjected into your homeschool in any way you see fit. As an example, I'll give you a brief look into how we typically integrate projects. One example was included in the beginning of this chapter where the gifted child was asked to experiment and catalog rocks and minerals on her own following a family lesson on the subject. Besides simple opportunities such as this, I usually incorporate projects following a study that has taken a length of time, such as a unit study. As an example, I'll give you a brief look into how we typically integrate projects after a lengthy study.

When Do You Start?

By the time my children are 7, they are introduced to the world of projects. I always complete the first projects alongside them. Once I see they're capable of completing a thorough project without my help, I'll be available as a resource for questions or ideas. By the time they're in fifth grade (hopefully earlier), they're expected to complete projects on their own with very little direction from me.

If you're starting projects when your child is older, I still suggest working alongside her at first and giving very clear expectations for final outcomes until she is able to complete a thorough project on her own.

When I say "give very clear expectations," this is a little misleading. I typically give my children expectations that are open-ended. In other words, "I expect your diorama to show at least five important aspects of Native American life. I also expect that all surfaces with be covered and several 3-D models will be present." This gives students direction without telling them exactly what to include and how to include it.

Where Do Projects Fit Into the Curriculum?

Most of the time our projects are interjected into unit studies or independent studies. (Although they could be used as additions or replacement to textbook assignments as well.) At the end of a period of learning, I decide how many projects are warranted. For instance, if a unit study has taken a long time and was in-depth, I'll expect more projects to be completed than a study that was very short. When we learned about Slavery and the Civil War for 12 weeks, I wanted to be sure the projects reflected both the time spent and the scope of material covered. For this unit, then, my children had to complete five different projects. Comparatively, we only spent a week investigating the subject of magnetism, so only one final project was assigned. Typically, my children have a length of time to complete the projects after the study has been completed. When working on the five projects at the end of our Slavery and Civil War study, they were given 2 weeks in which to do everything necessary to complete and present all five projects. After the magnetism study, they were only given 2 days to complete and present the final project.

Although you may certainly add or subtract from the guidelines below, you might find the following schedule of projects in Figure 7 helpful when considering how many are appropriate for varying lengths of study.

Length of Study	Number of Projects
1-2 Weeks	1-2 Projects
3-4 Weeks	2-3 Projects
5-6 Weeks	3-4 Projects
7-10 Weeks	4-5 Pojects
11-12 Weeks	5-6 Projects

Figure 7: How Many Projects Should I Assign?

How Do You Assign Projects?

For self-motivated children, I allow great freedom in choosing projects. For mom-motivated children, I will usually come up with a list of several project ideas from which they can choose. While varying the learning styles required for each project so they can do things that meet their desires, I also set the choices so they have to build certain skills. For example, if I know one of my children needs to work on writing skills, his project choices will be varied, but all will involve writing on some level. In an instance where I'm expecting him to complete and present two projects, I might offer these options:

- a file folder report,
- a skit with siblings,
- a blog post,
- a newspaper article, and
- an advertisement poster.

You can see that I've not only provided him with several varied choices that could meet a variety of learning preferences (e.g., research, drawing, acting, interpersonal, intrapersonal, technical writing, non-technical writing, handwriting, typing), but all involve writing on some level. Therefore, he gets to feel like he's mostly in control of his learning, while I know any of the choices he makes meet his need for getting more writing into his school time.

> **homeschool hint**
>
> In the end, you can choose to grade the projects if you like. Whether grading or not, I always talk with my children about what was good and what can be improved next time. Through gentle direction, my children have quickly learned how to critique their own work, too.

Of everything we do in our home, project-based learning has by far been the best tool to encourage independent learning and outstanding outcomes! And, it's the perfect tool for teaching my children similar topics, while allowing for individualized instruction (without a great deal of planning the differentiation on my part.)

Differentiation – whether it comes in the form of giving your gifted child something different to do than your other children, or venturing away from a textbook assignment to meet your child's needs better – is both important and beneficial. Your child will flourish when given instruction that matches her needs perfectly. Don't feel overwhelmed if you are new at individualizing instruction. Start with small changes. Assign something only mildly different from the other children or change only one part of a textbook assignment at first. Once you get the hang of it, differentiating won't be difficult at all!

Chapter 7

Organizing Your Homeschool Day and Record Keeping

One of the most frequently asked questions I get from new homeschoolers is, "How should we organize our school day?" To be quite honest, there is no right answer to this question. One family will follow a completely different schedule than another, but both of them will be successful in homeschooling. Why? Because each schedule fits the particular family's needs, in turn making it the perfect schedule for them.

As you think about how to schedule your days, weeks and school year, you'll want to consider such things as:

- *Work schedules.* Think about both the parent's and child's (if she's old enough) work schedules. If both parents work, for example, homeschool might be scheduled in the evening and on the weekends. Or, if your teenager works every day from 1 p.m. to 4 p.m., school might need to begin very early in the morning.

- *Outside commitments.* Homeschoolers are notoriously active in sports, co-ops, church, music lessons, drama practice, and other activities and must take these schedules into account when planning the rest of the school time.
- *Family patterns.* If you are a family of night owls, you may not want to schedule school to begin at 8 a.m. On the other hand, if you're up at the crack of dawn, you may choose to get started earlier.
- *Energy levels.* My children are morning workers and their "academic energy" drains quickly after lunch. Therefore, we do the heavy-duty learning of math and language arts early in the day and save the less academic things for later. One of my friends has very groggy morning learners and gets the most academically from her children only after the midday hour. We have both arranged our school days to get the most from our children, and although our days look nothing alike, they are both perfectly acceptable.
- *Neighbors and naptime.* If the neighbor children always show up at 3 in the afternoon to play, would you prefer to have school done before then? For a student with a younger sibling, is it easier for her to concentrate while the little one naps? These issues, and others like them, may not seem like a big deal, but you'll be surprised at how much better your day runs when they are taken into consideration.
- *Your yearly goals.* Do you want to complete school in 180 days, or it is okay with you to do ½ days once in a while and complete school in 220 days? Or, would you be more comfortable teaching all year round with four-day weeks? Does your child like to study in 2 or 3 month spurts, with large breaks in between? Would you like to schedule seasonal breaks such as fall/spring break or a Christmas vacation? Using a year-at-a-glance calendar will be helpful as you think about scheduling breaks and making sure you've included as many school days as your state requires.
- *Big breaks.* If possible, plan ahead for breaks you might need to take for a pregnancy, surgery, hosting company, and the like. Preplanning breaks and having a plan in mind for starting school again will

motivate you to get back into the swing of things in a reasonable amount of time.

I hope all these factors and possibilities don't frustrate you as you begin to think about organizing your days, weeks and years. Rather, I hope you see how wonderfully flexible homeschooling really is. As I mentioned earlier when talking about finding curriculum, don't expect to find your perfect schedule right away. And, once you do find a schedule that fits your family well, don't be surprised when some new, wonderful opportunity rolls around to throw a monkey wrench into it!

For most children, some semblance of a schedule is better than none at all. Even if you're trying to be a very flexible teacher and allow your child plenty of academic freedoms, she will likely thrive under at least a general daily or weekly plan.

On the other hand, when a schedule becomes too rigid, school can become stale fast – for both the parent and the child. I've known many homeschool parents who had a wonderfully organized daily schedule planned out for which every fifteen minutes was accounted. If their children took too long to complete an assignment, they were all in a tizzy because of being off schedule. If their children completed an assignment early, they found the kids became extremely bored and lost focus waiting to get back on the schedule. You may think such rigid planning sounds rather silly, but more parents than you can imagine fall into this trap. Why? Well, schools schedule classes and move on to the next subject at a specified time, right? Why shouldn't a homeschool do the same thing? And, it would be extremely easy to count all the hours for tracking, wouldn't it?

Remember that homeschooled children, gifted or not, will rarely take as long to complete an assignment as in a school setting. You, as the teacher, give one-on-one instruction and your child gets right to work, meaning the lessons are completed rather quickly. That's one end of the argument against timed schedules. On the other end, if we're going to allow children some freedoms and independence in learning, then a timed schedule will only serve to drive a child crazy. When he's ready to immerse himself into a certain topic, he needs nothing less than you pointing at your watch telling him, "Time's up!"

In order to give my children a general schedule without being too rigid, I opt for a daily plan that is *very* flexible when needed. Our normal daily schedule looks something like that in Table 7.

Table 7. My Daily Schedule	
Bible and Morning Time	Our day generally begins with Bible around the breakfast table. Afterwards, we do a small handful of starter activities that might include quick games, flashcards, poetry, memory work, puzzles, or current events.
Morning Chores	Our school day goes better when the house is tidy. Everyone is expected to help with chores before the school day begins.
Math	Because math requires a sharp mind and my children are the sharpest in the morning, we begin the day with math. There is no set time frame to be finished.
Language Arts	Once math is completed, my children move on to language arts. This can include any one or more of the following, depending on the day's schedule: grammar, spelling, handwriting, phonics, reading, research, or writing. I would almost never schedule all of these in one day. Again, there is no set time frame for these to be finished.
Science and/or History	Because science and history interest my children so much, these are subjects they look forward to studying. The promise of science or history time spurs them on to complete the more monotonous work of math and language arts.
Lunch	Lunches are very simple around our house and everyone gets about an hour to take a break and do whatever he or she pleases, including mom.
Extras	This time can include just about anything. If something needs to be finished from earlier in the day, it's taken care of first. Otherwise, we might take in a family chapter book, go on a nature walk, or play a board game.
Educational Free Time	Although my children do have what I call "complete" freedom during the day, this early afternoon free time is expected to be productive. My children may choose whatever they like, but it needs to be of some value like training horses, instrument practice, building, knitting, or baking.

Keep in mind this is a very general schedule which can easily change based on a project my children are working on, or a field trip, club meeting, or lesson that we plan to attend. In fact, when the general daily plan becomes too predictable, I purposely change it up with a field trip, game day, project day, or free choice day. This not only breaks up monotony, but keeps my children from settling into a single style of learning. In the future, they will meet many varied challenges, and I don't want something new, out of the ordinary, or challenging to throw them for a loop.

But, What If You Have a Dawdler?

A dawdler is a child who takes way too long to complete her work. She is entirely capable of the assignment, but instead chooses to waste time or tip-toe ever so slowly through the work.

Quite often, a dawdler is simply bored with the work, so giving something more challenging or more in line with her learning style might solve the problem. Sometimes, a dawdler does well when a parent works alongside (or even just sits alongside) her while the work is being completed. For a dawdler who is more stubborn and simply doesn't care about completing an assignment no matter the efforts you take to make it more interesting, I suggest using an egg timer.

real-life example

In my home, when the dawdler rears its ugly head, my children know I mean business when the egg timer comes out. I decide on a reasonable amount of time for the completion of an assignment and set the egg timer. My children know that if they aren't finished (or at least very close to being finished), I will give them another assignment in the same subject. If that means they spend 8 hours doing grammar, so be it. Yes, it sounds harsh, but it rarely takes more than once or twice before my children know that dawdling isn't acceptable.

I've found that most gifted kids are happy to complete assignments that interest them, but can be quite persnickety when uninterested in a subject or assignment. Unfortunately, even the uninteresting things need to be done, and the egg timer trick has worked well as a motivator. Just be sure you don't confuse a dawdler with a child actually having difficulty with an assignment.

When a child *is* having difficulty completing an assignment in a reasonable amount of time in spite of working hard or is struggling to complete the work correctly, it's probably time to slow down. If he understands the material, but takes way too long to complete the lesson, consider assigning smaller portions.

real-life example

> My children use Saxon Math, which is a clear, concise, and challenging program, but the lessons offer a lot of practice work. I found that asking my children to complete every single problem was taking up half of our morning just to get through math. Realizing that the odd and even problems work on the same skills, I now allow my children to work through either the odd or even problems. They still score well on lessons and tests while we use our time more efficiently.
>
> Another example of assigning smaller portions comes courtesy of my son who prefers not to write. When he was younger, to assign him a research paper or creative writing assignment as a whole project would surely have sent him to his final resting place. Instead, I gave him the whole picture of what I expected in the final project, but assigned him very small portions to complete each day. One day, for instance, you would have found him brainstorming ideas. Another day, he might have drawn some pictures of the ideas floating through his mind about the writing. The next day I would ask him to write an outline. Over the following 3 days, he was expected to write just one page of a three-page essay. Next, we would work on editing together, which left him only one last step of rewriting the final draft. Yes, one paper would take him at least 2 weeks to write, meaning he didn't end the school year with a thick folder full of writing samples. However, he *had* written, learned the process, and done so with far more joy and confidence than if I had simply assigned seemingly insurmountable writing assignments and left him to tackle them blindly.

Another reason to slow down is for a child who simply struggles to understand a concept. So many parents worry that taking 2 or 3 days to complete one lesson in a textbook will put their children too far behind, so they push to complete lessons whether or not the child really understands the material. This is such a tragedy. Taking extra time to review, reteach, or teach in a different way will benefit your child far more in the long run than completing every single lesson. Slow and steady wins the race for the struggling child.

real-life example

> In first grade, my son was not reading well. I pushed lesson after lesson in our reading and phonics books thinking surely more work would equal a great reader. By the end of the first semester, I knew he was losing the desire to become a reader. It wasn't fun anymore, and he felt the pressure to be a reader because I was way too tense wondering what was wrong with this child. Because we are a family of readers, I didn't want him to grow to hate reading, so I stopped all reading and phonics lessons for the remainder of the year. Reading once again became a cozy, loving time of mom simply reading aloud from good books.
>
> As he entered the second grade, I decided to try again with reading and phonics lessons. This time he was physically, mentally, and academically ready to learn to read. In no time, he was reading – and reading well. His fluency, comprehension, and ability levels quickly improved to grade level. In other words, just because we took time to slow down and work with him where he was at the time, didn't mean he was doomed to be behind forever. In fact, *because* I allowed him to work at his own pace without condemnation, he is now a very good reader who loves to relax with a good book. If I had kept pushing, I doubt reading (or any language arts subject) would be tackled so well today.

Record-Keeping

Record keeping for the gifted homeschooling child can get a little trickier than just checking off boxes that certain curricula or subjects have been taught each day. If he's spent 3 weeks immersed in the study of aeronautics and done little else, how do you record that? If he's only doing traditional textbook work two days a week and running from debate team and choir to basketball and Latin class with library time and visiting the nursing home in between, you can't keep simple records.

Because of state requirements, record keeping is a must for most homeschoolers. The records you keep prove that you are homeschooling legally should anyone ever want to know. They also serve as remembrances for you if writing report cards is one of your requirements. Most parents also find that keeping detailed records leaves wonderful reminders when the time comes to complete transcripts or list achievements or experiences on a resume.

Because most of us won't homeschool in a way in which boxes can be checked off, we have to be a little creative in record keeping. I'll detail my record keeping plan to give you an example of out-of-the-box recording, but do what works for your family, while meeting your state's requirements at the same time.

I keep a three-ring binder full of lined notebook paper in which to write our learning each week. I write the headings of "language arts," "math," "science," "history/social studies/geography," "Bible," and "other" on one page for each child. When my son completes a grammar lesson, reads a book, works on a research paper, writes in his journal, gives a speech, and so on, it gets written under the language arts section on his page. If he happens to be working on a history project that includes a timeline of the Civil War in which he had to do research on the computer, I might include that under history, language arts, math and other (computer skills) – if the project took a good deal of time to complete. Classes, clubs, service projects, church events, field trips, and other activities are all included on the weekly recording page, too. A sample recording page is included in Figure 8.

Figure 8. Sample Recording Page

Dates: Feb. 1-7	Week: 24/36
<u>Language Arts</u>	<u>Science</u>
Read (1) chapter book	Apologia biology lessons with labs |||
Wrote in journal	Biology dissection at co-op
Revised Civil War biography of Robert E. Lee	Prepared volcano experiment for brother
Completed Civil War timeline ||	Watched DVD about ocean animals
Researched Civil War soldier camps online	<u>History/Social Studies/Geography</u>
(2) vocabulary pages from workbook	Read (2) Civil War books
Latin/Greek flashcards with brother	Wrote personal narrative about life as Civil War nurse in journal (A)
Read from Bible ||||	Presented biography of Robert E. Lee (A-)
Read to preschool brother |||	Completed Civil War timeline (A)
(2) spelling workbook pages ||	Researched Civil War soldier camps
Grammar workbook pages ||||	Visited site of Civil War battle in Frankfort
Fallacy Detective lesson	Viewed Civil War displays at KY History Center
Public speaking – biography of Robert E. Lee	Watched documentary of Civil War on PBS
Listened to book on tape about Civil War	Listened to historical fiction book on tape
	Mapped various Civil War battles
<u>Math</u>	<u>Other</u>
Saxon lesson ||| (Averaged 23/24)	Animal Care
(4) logic puzzlers	Babysitting
Civil War timeline	Chores
Doubled and prepared (2) recipes for potluck	Volunteered at ballgame
Helped me balance checkbook	Music class at co-op
Practiced preschool math skills with brother ||	Planned meals and shopping list for the week
Critical Thinking class at co-op	Cleaned out stalls at barn
Worked concessions at ballgame	Helped grandmother clean basement
Couponing	
<u>Bible</u>	
Read from Bible ||||	
Prepared lesson on prayer for Sunday School	
Attended church and youth group	
Recited (5) memory verses	
Christian Character class at co-op	

At the end of the week, I look to see that each section is weighted with plenty of learning experiences. If not, I might encourage a little more time in the lesser areas in the weeks to come. I've found that most weeks end with the areas weighted pretty evenly since so many assignments and activities incorporate more than one subject.

> **homeschool hint**
>
> These weekly recordings also serve as my required attendance record, as well as my report card reminders. I simply jot the dates down each week as a record that my children were in attendance on those days. When I'm required to write a report card every 9 weeks, I use the pages to sum up what my children have accomplished and determine grades. (I usually note any relevant grades beside the assignments on the notebook pages.) As I look over the previous 9 weeks, I consider if there is anything we need to work on and make goals for the next reporting term, too.

Throughout the entire year, I save all tangible work and make lists of the non-tangible things. The non-tangible lists include books my children have read, field trips taken, service projects completed, and descriptions of clubs and other learning opportunities. I also keep a folder of all awards or certificates of achievement. At the end of the year, I create a portfolio to serve as proof of our legitimate homeschool. When I need to prepare transcripts, the portfolios make my work easy.

homeschool toolbox

Each child's portfolio includes:

- a sampling of some of my children's best work. I try to save a few things in each subject and throw away the rest of it. They would do the same thing at school, so don't feel bad. Although, you may not want your child to watch you throw away their things. If you really struggle with putting things in the garbage can, you can certainly keep all of it. But, a better option would be taking pictures of the work and creating a photo journal to keep with the portfolio.;
- all awards and/or certificates of achievement;
- all report cards;
- any legal documents having to do with homeschooling during the year;
- all the recording sheets on which I noted what we did daily. (Remember, this includes my attendance record, too.); and
- all lists of curriculum used, books read, field trips taken, clubs attended, and so on.

In the end, I have a great final product that is useful for the future as well. At the same time, it required very little work to keep up with throughout the year. Of course, just like everything else in this book, there is no right way to keep records. Find a system that works for you. Also, like everything else, it may take some trial and error to find a system that makes you happy. Keep tweaking until you feel comfortable.

Chapter 8

What About Socialization?

I'm sure you've heard the concerns about homeschooling and its lack of socialization – it seems to be the hottest argument against homeschooling. At least 8 out of 10 questions I receive from non-homeschoolers about homeschooling are some form of, "What about socialization?" Most people can't imagine that there are appropriate opportunities for socializing outside of the typical classroom setting.

In reality, socialization is actually one of the greatest advantages of homeschooling, especially for gifted and twice-exceptional children who already struggle to fit in with the crowd. They get to experience socialization at appropriate times, take part in meaningful activities (usually with plenty of supervision), and there are often more choices for what to attend than even public school children have. As a rule, homeschoolers are a very accepting crowd, too. Because they are constantly around people of all ages, cultures, and abilities, it seems completely normal to welcome and befriend people of all types. Additionally, gifted students don't simply have age peers, but intellectual and interest peers, too (Fonseca, 2011). In all my experiences homeschooling, neither my children or I have ever felt a lack of socialization or slighted by our choices in any way.

In fact, when answering the inevitable socialization question, although very polite in my answer, I'm thinking things in my head such as:

1. Whoever made the rule that socialization was most appropriate within very strict age limitations? Why can't my children be friends with people from ages 1-100?
2. Since when is school the best place for socializing? Shouldn't the students be learning instead?
3. Why should I be content to socialize my 6-year-old with other children who will inevitably teach him about "unsavory" topics before he's ready to learn about them?
4. Because socialization and peer pressure are fairly synonymous terms as related to most school settings, why would I want my child to feel obligated to live up to someone else's standards?

These questions are true of all children, but more magnified when speaking of gifted kids. Many of them already feel the pressure of being "different." If they work grade levels ahead or can carry on masterful conversations, kids their age can't keep up. If they have fantastic creative abilities, but get in trouble often because they can't sit still, other children shy away from them. Examples of gifted children not fitting in could go on and on, but I'm sure you don't really need me to keep writing because you've probably already seen signs of this yourself.

Would you believe homeschooling is socially more like real life than that of a classroom setting? As an adult, can you remember a time where you have been asked to do something with people who are within one year of your age? Probably not. You live, work, worship, volunteer, shop, attend events, and even play sports with a large variety of ages. And, one of the beautiful facets of multi-age activities is that younger or less experienced people learn from older or more experienced people. The same is true of homeschoolers. They have many, many more opportunities to be part of multi-age events, and in turn, become part of the "real" world more quickly (Klicka, 2007).

Unfortunately, social stigmas are part of life for almost every gifted and twice-exceptional child in the school system. Many kids are given labels such as learning disabled, dyslexic, and ADHD. Even the term *gifted* carries negative connotations in some situations. Worse are the labels given by other children such as freak, weirdo, brainiac, geek, or nerd. And, no matter how hard we as parents try to encourage our child against defining himself based on outside labels, it's hard. Labels stick like glue in the mind of a child, especially when the class bully so lovingly and constantly reminds the child of his place.

Parents of homeschoolers, on the other hand, are in the driver's seat of labeling. Although I'm not promising that your child will never be called a bad name, you are the person who gets to define who he is. Your loving, encouraging words and lack of labeling will keep him from seeing his giftedness as something out of the ordinary. For, you see, it *is* ordinary for him to be the way he is! Additionally, you are in the driver's seat for friendships and other social experiences. Unlike at school, if a certain homeschool group is full of bullies, you don't have to keep attending.

Morality is another social advantage of homeschooling. Homeschooled kids who attend social events are there because they want to be and/or their parents want them to be. In other words, there is usually a motivation for going other than, "The government says I have to be here, but, by golly, I don't have to like it and I don't have to behave!" These events are typically well monitored by parents and/or teachers, and quite often consist of small groups of children. In most cases, a particular group only meets once per week or month. For these reasons, the children don't have to deal with as many moral conundrums like gossip, pressure to have premarital relations in the bathroom between classes, or friends who want them to sneak a drink of alcohol hiding in the locker.

Don't get me wrong, homeschooling doesn't mean you won't have to deal with moral issues. Simply, your children will likely have fewer opportunities to be coaxed into immorality. Also, because of the nature of homeschooling, you will have more time to impress your family's beliefs and code of behavior upon your child, too, making it much easier for him to know what decisions to make when the times come.

Believe it or not, some people actually claim the above issue to be a disadvantage of homeschooling. People often tell me that I'm sheltering my children and they need to learn how to be bullied, to be faced with the tough moral decisions as children, and so on. They try to convince me that my "sheltering" will only set them up for failure in adulthood. True, there are adult bullies to contend with, and morality issues face us all on a daily basis. However, walking alongside my children with love, encouragement, and training allows them a safe place to land when making inevitable mistakes. Providing them with plenty of social opportunities in which I'm still in the driver's seat is what I call responsible parenting. As they are ready to step into the driver's seat as adults, I trust that my example and training will go a long way in helping them to face bullies and temptations with confidence and grace, rather than fear and frustration.

Just What Does a Socialized Homeschooler Look Like?

That answer varies widely depending on so many factors. Is your child an introvert or an extrovert? How often do you believe your child needs to be with other people? In what is your child interested? What's available in your area? Does your child prefer to take a class or serve the community? How much money do you have to spend? How much time do you have?

You see, you could literally do anything and everything under the sun as a homeschooler. Your problem won't be finding opportunities to socialize; it will be reining yourself or your children into a reasonable amount of wonderful opportunities!

Homeschool Groups

What are the basic group structures? As you read over this information, realize that no two groups are ever exactly the same.

- Play groups meet casually for the purpose of allowing children to play while parents talk. These groups meet at parks, churches, gyms, and in people's homes. They meet anywhere from once or twice a week to monthly. There is usually no fee unless the use of the building is charged. Since these groups are casual, there is no obligation to attend every meeting.
- Co-ops, otherwise known as cooperatives, generally gather once a week for the purpose of offering a variety of class choices to your child. They meet at churches, in community buildings, and in people's homes, depending on their size. Some co-ops divide children into age groups, others divide them by interest groups. Most of the time, the parent is expected to help occasionally. Fees vary greatly. Some groups charge per child, some per class, some per family, and some per expenses. Because the classes are typically ongoing for a semester or school year, you should make every effort to attend a co-op each time it meets.
- Clubs also come in many shapes and sizes, so it's impossible to give a concise explanation. They are generally groups of people interested in meeting for a specific purpose. Some examples include book discussion clubs, unit study clubs, science experiment clubs, 4-H clubs, drama clubs, and debate clubs. Sometimes, they will be offered through a homeschool support group, but you will also find them as standalone groups or through community programs such as the library and county extension office. Fees, meeting places, and age groupings vary greatly.
- At the moment, I'm part of a casual field trip group. All of the families are members of a private Facebook group and whenever one of us wants to plan and organize a field trip, we simply start a thread in the group informing the rest of the members about the plans. Often, if you're part of a co-op or other homeschool support group, there is someone designated to plan field trips.

Finding an appropriate group or club for your family takes just a little bit of investigative work. Most state homeschooling groups maintain a webpage of all the support groups available in the state. You should be able to find several nearby options with contact information or website addresses for more information. If one group doesn't sound like what you're looking for, ask the contact if she can point you in a better direction. Homeschool leaders are generally very helpful and won't mind talking with you even though you don't plan to take part in their group. A simple online search of your county or city and state with the term "homeschool" should bring up nearby options, too, if you don't seem to be finding anything otherwise.

Watch the newspaper for opportunities of all kinds. Request to be on mailing lists for museums, zoos, nature centers, aquariums, children's museums, history museums, recreation leagues, and more. They will keep you up-to-date on all their various classes and other offerings. Sign up on homeschool email lists or request to be a Facebook fan to keep up with new classes, field trips, and other exciting events. Talk to your local library and extension office to learn of upcoming classes and community events. Speak with your church leadership for homeschooling leads and youth happenings. Some public school districts and private schools allow homeschoolers to participate in extra-curricular activities. Contact the boards of education to find out if any of these activities would benefit your child.

Below, I've given you several common socialization opportunities for homeschoolers, but the lists are by no means all-inclusive. Let your mind (or your child's) take you wherever it may.

Socialization Through Clubs, Classes or Other Teaching Groups

4-H

Academic contest – spelling bee, geography bee, science fair, public speaking, etc.

An apprenticeship, internship, or other job

Book discussion club

Choir

Church

Club – robotics, science, Lego, nature, etc.

Community college class

Community gardening

Community play

Co-op class

Field trip with friends or groups

Girl Scouts or Boy Scouts

Jr. Historical Society

Keepers at Home or Contenders of the Faith

Musical ensemble

Other class – art, music, drama, photography, dance, sewing, etc.

Serving on a leadership board for a youth council

Sports – recreational league, bowling league, hiking group, etc.

Summer camp

YMCA or other athletic club

Socialization Through Volunteering

Be part of a trash pick-up team

Clean cages at an animal shelter

Help at a local Ronald McDonald House or someplace similar

Help organize or work during a community event

Offer to complete yard work or another task for an elderly neighbor or family member

Prepare a meal for a sick friend or new neighbor

Take part in a community or church work day

Visit a children's hospital to read books or play games with the children

Visit a nursing home regularly

Volunteer at a nature center or zoo

Volunteer to read to children at the local preschool or elementary school

Volunteer with Special Olympics

Work at the local soup kitchen or food pantry

Volunteer for a political campaign

Starting a Homeschool Group

What if nothing you find meets your needs and you'd like to form your own homeschool group? Go for it! Depending on the type of group you want to form, there are a few basic questions you'll need to ask yourself to ensure the group runs smoothly:

- *What type of group do I want and for what purpose?* A few common responses include:
    - My child needs play dates, so I'll organize a monthly meeting at the park.
    - I'd really like to start a small co-op so my child can have some other teachers once a week besides myself.
    - I can't find a local robotics club and my child really wants to take part, so I'll see if we can gather a few families for this purpose.
    - We love field trips, but don't like going by ourselves all the time. I'll gather several families and see if each parent would be willing to schedule one field trip per year for the group.

- *Do I need to consider a meeting place for the group?* Contact the library, extension office, and a few churches in the area to see if they are willing to donate the use of a room. If they won't donate the room, consider charging a small fee to the group members to cover the expense. When money is involved, it's a little harder to get people to commit, so you might consider a much smaller group that can meet in your home instead.

- *Who will I invite and how will I get the word out?* Once you've formed a vision for the group and know you have a meeting place, it's time to start thinking about who you will invite. Will you invite just a few close friends or the entire homeschooling community? How will you communicate with people? Will you need to advertise in the newspaper or through other homeschool support groups? Will you open a group Facebook group or start a website? (If it's going to be a big group, you should probably consider pulling a few close friends together to help you think through the organization of the group.)

- *What do I need to make this group happen?* Will you need to contact, and potentially hire, teachers? Will you need to round up volunteers for teaching or supervising? Will the group need any supplies and how will they be purchased?

- *What will it cost?* Think of this from both your perspective and that of the others involved. If you're just organizing a casual field trip group, does there need to be a $10 limit on planned activities? If you're starting a robotics club, will you purchase the materials or ask the involved families to split the cost? Parents will want to know what they get from the group and what it will cost in the very beginning.

- *How long will the group meet?* Most homeschoolers don't like to make long term commitments. There are just too many great opportunities available to be tied down to one thing too long. For groups that will meet weekly, think realistically about how long you can keep the attention of the children and plan an ending date. If everyone is still gung-ho to continue by the end, you can always schedule another session. Of course, groups that only meet once a month for such things as field trips or play dates can go on until they run their course. You'll know when it's time to move on.

- *Will I need to develop any rules?* Some groups like to nip problems in the bud early. Consider if you need to make rules about late payments, attendance, dress codes, behavior, or the like before starting the class. More formal groups usually put these rules in writing and ask new members to sign a copy stating they understand and agree to abide by the rules.

Let your child's interests lead the way when organizing a social or academic group. Just in case you need some ideas for clubs or classes, I've compiled an exciting list of possibilities in Table 8.

Table 8. Ideas for Homeschool Group Classes

ACT/SAT Prep	American Gov't	Art History	Babysitting	Bible Drill
Cake Decorating	Candle Making	Car Care	Career Planning	Carpentry
Ceramics	Chess	Choir	Christian Characater	Computer Skills
Cooking	Creative Ministries	Cross-Stitch	Dance	Debate
Decoupage	Drama	Drawing	Electrical Engineering	Entrepreneurship
Etiquette	Financial Responsibility	Firt Aid/CPR	Flower Arranging	Foreign Language
Forensics	Gardening	Geography/ Cultures	Group Music Lessons	History Themes
Jewelry Making	Kitchen Chemistry	Knitting or Crochet	Leather Works	Lego
Logic	Math Games	Metal Working	Missionary Studies	Musical Theater
Mysteries	Nature	Oratory	Painting	PE
Photography	Reader's Theater	Reading Discussion	Robotics	Science Labs
Scrapbooking	Sculpting	Self-Defense	Sewing	Sign Language
Soap Making	State History	Web Design	Wood Working	Writing

Parents are the best options for teaching classes because they will usually teach for free. Find out what talents and training other homeschooling parents have and see if they would be willing to teach a short-term or long-term class. A local business might be willing to lend an employee for a short-term class for free or for a small fee. Extension agents love to teach classes of all sorts. Call on retired teachers who are not only experts in their field, but might be more than happy to donate their time or teach inexpensively. Retired people in general often love to be asked to share their expertise with homeschool groups.

Socialization Statistics

As you can see, homeschoolers do not lack for socialization opportunities. And, after reading through this chapter, I doubt you really need statistical evidence to prove the positive socialization of homeschoolers. But, if you do, there are plenty of studies to be found. The Homeschool Legal Defense Association has written an article titled "Socialization: Homeschoolers Are in the Real World" (Klicka, 2007) that cites much of the best research currently available on the topic of homeschoolers, socialization, and self-esteem. You might also be interested in reading *The Well-Adjusted Child: The Social Benefits of Homeschooling* by Rachel Gathercole for further information.

chapter 9

Thinking About College

College planning is a big concern for all homeschoolers for the simple fact that potential careers are on the line and there are certain requirements that must be met before most colleges will consider accepting a student. When you throw in the potential for early entrance into college for gifted students, the considerations increase. I'll ease your fears right off the bat by telling you that getting into college is no harder for homeschoolers than those in the school system. The only difference is that much of the legwork will be on your end because you won't have a school counselor to guide you. However, there are dozens of wonderful books available detailing the process from start to finish. They will serve to encourage, give you clear planning steps as early as the middle school years, and give you how-to tips and checklists to make the process as smooth as possible.

homeschool toolbox

Books about college prep during the high school years:

- *College-Prep Homeschooling: Your Complete Guide to Homeschooling Through High School* by David P. and Chandra Byers
- *Homeschoolers' College Admissions Handbook: Preparing Your 12- to 18-Year-Old for a Smooth Transition* by Cafi Cohen
- *Homeschooling: The Teen Years: Your Complete Guide to Successfully Homeschooling the 13- to 18-Year-Old* by Cafi Cohen
- *Senior High: A Home Designed Form+U+La* by Barbara Edtl Shelton
- *The Ultimate Guide to Homeschooling Teens* by Debra Bell

Books about creating transcripts and getting into college:

- *College Planning for Gifted Students: Choosing and Getting Into the Right College* (3rd ed.) by Sandra L. Berger
- *Free College Resource Book* by Doug Hewitt and Robin Hewitt
- *Get Into College in 3 Months or Less* by Doug Hewitt and Robin Hewitt
- *Setting the Records Straight: How to Craft Homeschool Transcripts and Course Descriptions for College Admissions and Scholarship* by Lee Binz
- *Transcripts Made Easy: The Homeschooler's Guide to High School Paperwork* by Janice Campbell

If you aren't quite ready to think about the nitty-gritty of getting your child into college just yet, here's the bottom line. You need to know your state's requirements for college-bound high school graduates *and* learn what some of your potential college choices require. Begin looking into these requirements as early as middle school so you can chart the high school coursework early and not have last-minute surprises. Additionally, many gifted students will be able to fulfill some of the requirements earlier than ninth-twelfth grades, leaving room for higher level studies, apprenticeships, or even possible early admission to college.

You will want to keep detailed records of classes, hours, and grades as you begin high-school-level courses for the purpose of completing a final transcript. Detailed notes about clubs, leadership positions, performances, service projects, work experiences, and the like will be important, too, as you begin filling out college entrance forms. Keep copies of awards and publications of your child's work, and attain letters of recommendation from anyone willing to attest to her competencies from their perspective. Keep all of these records organized in one place so they are at the ready when you need them.

When you begin to think more seriously about college and need to know which exams to take and when, how to get financial aid or scholarships, when to make college visits and how to fill out applications, you will want to read at least one of the books listed above. The earlier you can read up on the subject, the smoother the entire process will be.

Should Gifted Children Consider Early Entrance Into College?

Some gifted students are going to be so far ahead in typical studies before twelfth grade, that they may be academically ready for college classes early. Although there are some colleges and universities that have early entrance programs for gifted students, these are few and far between. That doesn't mean other colleges won't accept younger students, but the task of gaining entrance may be full of more hoops, paperwork, interviews, testing, and coaxing.

Whether your child is ready for college courses at 16 or 6, there are several things to consider. First, and foremost, is your child emotionally ready for courses at the college level? Not necessarily whether or not your child can handle the course work, but can she handle the environment that goes along with attending college? Her classmates most likely will be older and may or may not appreciate her presence in their classes. Likewise, not all professors will like the idea of teaching younger students and may make life somewhat difficult in response. Many older college students will talk about adult issues and escapades, while some course material may be very adult in nature, too. Additionally, college courses require a level of independence, responsibility, and organization that are bumped up a notch, while class material is covered at an accelerated pace. And not to be forgotten, college costs money.

On the flip side, many gifted children who enter college early thrive. Those who have always preferred adult conversation find themselves comfortable. Those who never found a group of people intensely interested in their favorite subject find classes full of people who are also passionate. Those who need to be challenged while the parents have run out of challenging resources find highly trained professors who meet their needs.

Among the more obvious considerations already listed, you will also need to think about such things as:

- Does my child really want to go to college, or am I pushing the issue because I know his potential?
- Will my child be able to live at home? If not, is she emotionally ready for the detachment? Am I emotionally ready for the detachment?
- If my child isn't driving, how will he get to and from classes?
- What will I do if the college requires me to sit in on the classes or remain close by?
- Can she handle the organization required, or will I have to make sure she's completing the assignments?

homeschool hint

As you can see, the decision whether or not to enter full-time college early will need to be weighed carefully. However, when you take the time to do your research and find a college that matches your child's needs, early entrance can be very fulfilling and fruitful.

Some parents may worry that their gifted child is academically ready for college, but has not necessarily completed every prerequisite. For instance, he writes stories for publication at the age of 12 with perfect grammar and style, but has never actually taken an English class. Remembering that you are the homeschool teacher and can design your own courses in most instances, you can compile his writings and a notation of their publications, and count that toward and English credit on the transcript. You might also be surprised that some colleges will allow an incoming student to test out of certain prerequisites, eliminating the need to fret over not actually covering the material. An interesting book on this subject that you might like to read is *College without High School: A Teenager's Guide to Skipping High School and Going to College* by Blake Boles.

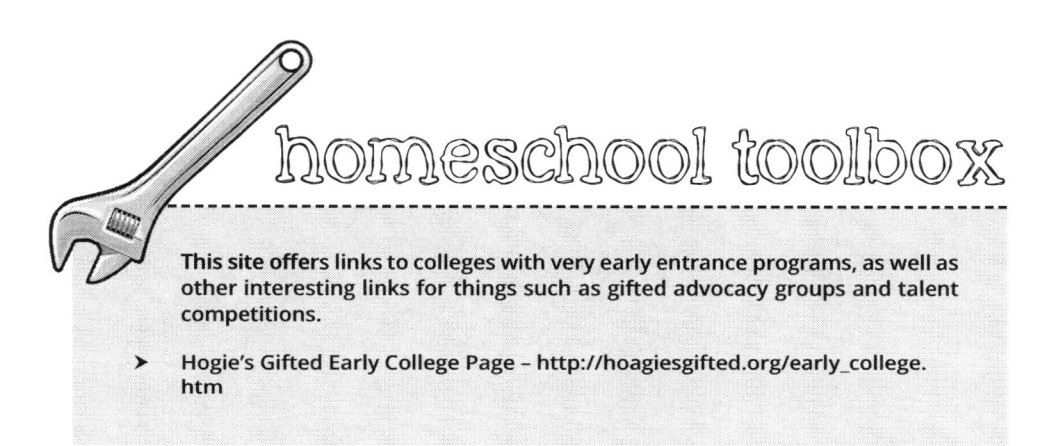

homeschool toolbox

This site offers links to colleges with very early entrance programs, as well as other interesting links for things such as gifted advocacy groups and talent competitions.

- Hogie's Gifted Early College Page – http://hoagiesgifted.org/early_college.htm

What If My Child Isn't Ready for Full-Time Early Entrance Into College?

There are several other viable options to consider rather than full-time entry into college at an early age:

- If you, someone you know, or a tutor has expertise in a particular subject area, it's likely that college level courses can be taught at home. Although your child may not get college credit for this type of class, he will be challenged, while attaining valuable accelerated learning for his college future. Anytime your child can take an accelerated course, it looks fantastic on the high school transcript. Such classes may make it easier to get into a desired college *and* attain a nice scholarship.

- If your child is capable of independent learning, you can purchase college-level textbooks for her to study on her own. Some colleges, like MIT (ocw.mit.edu/courses), offer entire class lectures online for free. Again, while neither of these options count toward college credit, valuable higher level studies can keep advanced students satisfied.
- Many colleges offer distance-learning courses. Depending on the college, the classes may transfer once your child enters college full-time. Even if they won't transfer, this type of class at least requires a level of accountability that is great preparation for college. Also, someone else is the teacher, so you are somewhat off the hook in providing the challenging material.
- Entering into one or two community college courses which are close to home and don't require full-time admission into college is another option which many families of gifted learners utilize. Community colleges are popping up all over the place and are typically very willing to accept nontraditional students. In fact, high school students can often enroll into these classes for free or highly discounted rates. In many instances, they can also be considered dual-enrollment classes, meaning they can be counted on both the high school transcript and for college credit.
- If your child isn't quite ready for college courses for one reason or another, consider a year or two of apprenticeship in various areas of her learning passions.
- Rather than an apprenticeship, he could spend the extra time between the completion of high school and entering college to gain life experiences through traveling, working as a missionary, pursuing a dream like acting or singing, or taking part in serious competitions for gifted learners. A great source for finding competition opportunities is *Competitions for Talented Kids: Win Scholarships, Big Prize Money, and Recognition* by Frances A. Karnes and Tracy L. Riley. A good book for other college-preparatory ideas is *The Ultimate Guide to Summer Opportunities for Teens: 200 Programs That Prepare You for College Success* by Sandra Berger.

homeschool toolbox

As you consider the many college level options available, online support groups can be an encouragement for you and answer various questions you may have. The TAGMAX listserv group offers homeschooling advice of all kinds for parents who are homeschooling gifted children. Instructions for signing up for the listserv can be found at http://listserv.icors.org/scripts/wa-ICORS.exe?A0=TAGMAX.

No matter which options you choose to challenge your gifted learner as she becomes ready for college level classes, make sure she is on board with the decisions. Whichever path you take, not only will the learning will be challenging, but there's also a potential for life to become challenging, too. If she's in agreement about the choices made, there is a much better likelihood that success and joy will be found in the end.

Chapter 10

Frequently Asked Questions

Is My Child Actually Gifted? Should I Test Him?

There are so many aspects to giftedness such as high intelligence, extreme curiosity, well-developed reasoning skills, immense vocabulary, talent beyond teaching, and many more. Oftentimes, determining giftedness is strictly based on noticing characteristics or tendencies, while tests are given to measure intelligence quotients (IQ). From my perspective as a homeschooling mom of gifted kids, I don't see the necessity of testing for giftedness. Because I know exactly what my children are capable of and because I have intimate knowledge of their strengths and weaknesses, I don't really need a test to define what I already know. Even if I had test results, I wouldn't change how we homeschool because I already strive to meet their individual needs.

Testing would be more appropriate, in my opinion, if my children were in the school system so that I could advocate for appropriate learning environments. Our homeschool is already an appropriate learning environment, meaning tests would be a waste of our time and money.

If you really would like to have some definitive answers about the giftedness of your child or believe having "proof" will come in handy for future opportunities, there are several options for finding testers. A psychologist experienced with gifted children can administer IQ and achievement tests, as can public school or university psychologists. Most states have a gifted association that can point you in the direction of qualified testers, too.

What Do I Do if My Child Tells Me She Already Knows the Things I've Asked Her to Learn?

Ask her to prove it. You might assign a test from the end of a chapter or book, ask her to write a paper on the topic, expect a project of some sort to display her knowledge, or even have an in-depth discussion with her on the topic. If she truly does know it, move on. If not, maybe there are parts she can prove she understands so that less of the material has to be covered.

How Will I Know if My Kids are Keeping Up?

So many parents worry about this question. My first question to ask you in return is, "Who are you worried about keeping up with?" Are you hoping to keep up with the kids in fourth grade at your local school? If there are 24 children in the class, they are working on 24 different levels. Would you like to attain the fourth grade standards of public schools? Almost every school in every district in every state has different standards. Would you like to know your child can do the work in a grade leveled textbook? Choose a stack of textbooks and they will each expect different skills. Do you want to keep up with all the kids of the same age at your homeschool co-op? Each one of those children has different learning styles, gifts, and challenges.

My point is that there is no set standard that your child *must* meet. He should be steadily progressing in all subjects. Whether he's working three grade levels ahead of his age or one grade level behind, if you observe growth, don't worry about keeping up with anyone.

Of course, there are standardized tests which can help ease your fears if you really want to know that your child is keeping up. Just remember that those are based on typical skills for typical kids. Most gifted and twice-exceptional children are far from typical. Also, the final scores of standardized tests depend greatly on whether or not your child is a good test-taker. He could be brilliant, but not test well. You might know in your gut that he really is brilliant and can't figure out why such poor scores resulted. My advice is to go with your gut.

How Do I Keep My Gifted Child From Becoming Prideful About Her Intelligence or Talents?

As a parent, you must purposely work toward humility. Your child shouldn't hear all the time how wonderful and brilliant she is. I know that sounds harsh, but building character is not about boosting an ego. Of course we want our children to know they are talented and their talent shouldn't be wasted, but that same talent doesn't make her better than someone else with a different talent or a lesser talent than she.

In our family, we have encouraged humility through service opportunities. We are never happier than when our family collectively uses our talents to serve others. This can come in a variety of ways, but a few examples include:

- Gifted singers or musicians can perform for the nursing home.
- Talented mathematicians can help elderly neighbors file their taxes.

- Amazing chefs can make goodies for the soup kitchen.
- Outstanding readers can volunteer to read with children at an orphanage.

On the other side of the coin, you should never make one child feel less valued than another. Even if your other children are not gifted, they will have talents and interests that are just as important and should be nurtured and encouraged no differently than the highly gifted child. In the end, all of your children will feel special and be sent into the world with confidence to boldly go wherever their path leads them.

The same goes for your gifted kid who might, ahem, stand out in not-so-desirable ways. She shouldn't be made to feel less valued than the other children who aren't quite as active, inquisitive, intense, and so on. Character training is a key to any successful homeschool, but absolutely essential where gifted kids are involved. Teaching your children (and reminding yourself) about such things as patience, humility, peacefulness, kindness, and so on will go a long way in everyone being accepting of one another and his or her quirks.

My Child Battles from Negative Feelings After Having Been in School. How Can I Combat These?

This question can actually mean a few different things, all of which I hear frequently. First, some children see their giftedness as negative because of the way they've been treated by teachers or peers in school, in turn making them fight against wanting to grow in their giftedness. Second, some children hated school to begin with and have a negative attitude about schoolwork at home. Third, some children loved school and miss their friends, assignments, and/or the consistency.

If your child wasn't treated well in school, you're going to have the awesome task of boosting his self-confidence and building his self-worth. Your consistent, loving encouragement will go a long way in helping the negative thoughts fade away. Consider finding a homeschool group full of accepting kids and teachers to be around regularly, too. It would be especially nice to find a group of children who are also gifted in the same manner to encourage him to not be ashamed or afraid to grow in his talents. For instance, if your child recalls every piece of trivia that's ever passed by him, he might thrive well being part of a quick recall quiz team.

If your child hated school and wants no part of homeschooling either, my best advice is to ditch anything and everything seeming like school for a little while. Take some time to "de-school" by going on several interesting field trips, playing board games and card games as a family, reading aloud or listening to classic literature audiobooks, baking together in the kitchen, serving the community at nursing homes or clothing drives, going on nature walks, and even watching educational programs. You'll be surprised at how much academic schooling comes through such atypical lessons! Better yet, your child will slowly learn that school isn't something to hate, but rather a wealth of wonderful opportunities awaiting him. Before long, he will be ready to accept more book work and traditional lessons, but will likely want to continue the exciting learning, too.

If your child struggles with the transition from school to home because he actually loved school, your task is to win him over to homeschooling. De-schooling, as mentioned above, is one way to encourage a love for the new life of homeschooling. If he misses his friends, allow them to get together socially on weekends. Take part in lots of social opportunities with other homeschoolers so he begins to make a new set of friends quickly, too. If he misses his teachers, or having teachers besides you, enroll in a good co-op which will offer classes without overstepping you as a homeschooling parent. If he misses the consistency of the classroom environment, bring more consistency into your homeschool. There are actually kids who thrive on daily schedules and that's okay. In fact, these children make homeschooling very easy for the parent.

What Challenges Can I Expect as a Parent Homeschooling a Gifted Child?

Depending on the gifted child, there can be many challenges such as keeping her busy, meeting her high academic standards, dealing with temperament, understanding sensitivities, and working through social frustrations. Specific help-books about dealing with social, emotional and academic needs of a gifted child *and* homeschooling are hard to find. Additionally, you may be pressed from family, friends, and school systems who think your decision to homeschool is not wise. And, on the more practical side, homeschooling in general takes time, money, and flexibility.

All of these struggles are worth every bit of the effort to work through! Your child will gain skills and confidence in an environment that fits her and challenges her perfectly. You will simply have to tweak the advice from books, stand firm in your decision to homeschool, find supportive homeschooling friends to encourage you, and learn to live with some lifestyle changes for this season of your life. You won't regret it.

Homeschooling mom and author, Colleen Kessler, put it best when she told me, "I never know what to expect, but I know that my kids' asynchronous needs will be met. I can teach my three year old sign language, skip counting, letter blends, and more, all while training her to wash her hands when she uses the bathroom, and how to snap her clothes. My son can study astronomy with the Cleveland Astronomical Society as an honorary member (since you are supposed to be 12 to join), talk with NASA Glenn engineers about the Saturn-V, learn multiplication, and write short paragraphs (hopefully even a short story someday!), while mastering his handwriting skills. Homeschooling a gifted kid is the ultimate test in patience and flexibility, but it's also the ultimate testimony to joy in learning."

FREQUENTLY ASKED QUESTIONS

What Can I Expect to Realistically Accomplish in My Life While Homeschooling?

The answer greatly depends on three things: how organized you are, what additional homeschooling activities you participate in, and how independent your child is.

If you stay on top of household chores and don't leave school planning to the last minute, you'll feel much more freedom than the parent who is constantly trying to keep up and put out fires. And, obviously, the more activities you allow your child to participate in, the more time it will take. Additionally, if your child needs you to be with him during much of his schoolwork, you will have less time to accomplish other things.

In my home, I work hard to make sure the house is at least straightened before we ever start school. I also take time weekly (usually on Sunday afternoon) to make sure there is an outline of the schoolwork for the week ahead. I *try* to limit out outside activities to a weekly co-op and one other activity per week for each of my children. And, finally, I start very early encouraging independent work as much as possible. The younger the child, the more dependent they are on me, but I take advantage of every opportunity to train independence in schoolwork.

Even with all this, I still define myself wholly as a homeschool mom, for that's my main job. It takes time and effort. I do accomplish other things (like book writing for instance), but "me" time or time to accomplish bigger tasks must be purposely fit into the schedule. That's okay, though, because I wouldn't trade a minute of watching my kids learn. And, I will treasure forever the deep relationships that flourish because we spend so much time together.

Homeschooling the Gifted Child Can Be Messy, Literally. How Do You Deal with a House Full of Messes?
••

This is very true! Whether your gifted child is a walking, unorganized mess herself or not, all the wonderful projects that she dives into will likely be messy or create messes as they scatter across your house. What's a parent to do?

My best advice is to learn to deal with it – at least on some level. Homeschoolers in general have to get used to a less than pristine house. First and foremost, they're actually at home most of the time which equals more messes. Also, in order to encourage creativity and excitement in learning (as we all want to do), messes are part of the outcome.

In our home, we have daily chore time in the mornings and a quick pick-up in the afternoons, with deep cleaning done on Saturdays. Keeping the house in decent order daily through regular chores and straightening goes a long way in keeping messes under control. We also try to keep as many of the long-term projects as possible contained to the schoolroom. If you don't have a dedicated room available for working on and storing the messy stuff, think about clearing out a closet, cabinet, or space underneath a bed for keeping things out of sight when necessary.

I'm Not a Certified Teacher. Can I Really Teach My Children?
••

Yes, you can! Just because I have a master's degree in education doesn't mean I know everything, or even know how to teach everything. However, I have resources to help me – just like you do. What history topics should my children cover before graduating? There are lists galore available on the Internet. What if I have no clue how to teach the concept of fractions? I can buy a video course for math. What if I can't stand the thought of teaching biology dissection? I can attend a co-op that teaches that for me.

You see, between the Internet, library, curriculum companies, support groups, family members, friends, and community resources there are more helps and more opportunities than you can ever imagine. The biggest key is that you love your child more than anybody else in this world. You know his strengths, weaknesses, quirks, needs, and desires better than anybody. Who better to give him an education in the long run?

Cindy Downes has written a book called *The Checklist* (oklahomahomeschool.com/checklist.html) that covers all the "must teach" topics in every academic area for both elementary and upper level students. It's a great resource for those who like to "see" that most topics have been covered over the course of homeschooling. There is also a series of books titled *What Your __ Grader Needs to Know* by E. D. Hirsch which give a large listing of topics to be covered each year.

From my perspective, I will never be able to teach my children everything they need to know. Believe it or not, school systems won't either. If I prepare my children to know *how* to learn, no topic will be out of their reach. For this reason, I don't worry too much about learning gaps. Big learning gaps will make themselves evident and we will deal with them as needed. Small learning gaps can be filled in by my children as their needs arise.

We Don't Have a Lot of Money. Can I Still Homeschool Effectively?

You most certainly can try to homeschool as inexpensively as possible. Personally, I don't spend more than a few hundred dollars a year homeschooling. How do I do it?

- I borrow everything I can from the library.

- I shop used curriculum sales, which are offered in most communities around May or June each year.
- I shop yard sales and thrift stores for games, learning toys, art supplies, books, and more.
- I frequent library book sales.
- I search online for free curriculum in the form of unit studies for history or science and worksheets for grammar and vocabulary.
- I keep curricula to reuse with my younger children.
- I teach at a local co-op to save tuition fees.
- My homeschooling friends and I take turns teaching fun classes to our children for no charge.
- We utilize the 4-H program in our county.
- We attend inexpensive field trips and wait for homeschool specials on pricier trips.

What Are the Most Important Supplies to Have on Hand in Our Homeschool?

Although there are all sorts of wonderful supplies you *could* have on hand in your homeschool, there is only a small list of what I would consider absolute necessities:

- paper (lined, graph, plain, colored, construction);
- pencils, erasers, and a good pencil sharpener;
- a good work surface where your child can sit comfortably and write with good form;
- basic office supplies like scissors, tape, a stapler, and a hole punch;
- basic art supplies like crayons, colored pencils, markers, watercolors, liquid glue, and stick glue;
- basic reference supplies like a dictionary, thesaurus, and atlas; and

- at least one bookshelf where you can begin to grow a home library. (Purchase wonderful fiction, nonfiction, and reference books as you happen upon them at yard sales, curriculum sales, and thrift stores.)

That's about it for the must-haves, besides curriculum of course. Without going overboard, I have included a list below of other extra supplies that we find ourselves using regularly and would be nice to have if you are able:

- a computer where your child is free to use the word processing program, play software, and has the ability to be online when necessary. A computer attached to a printer is even better;
- a digital camera for both documenting school activities and allowing a child to create projects;
- large wall maps of the world and United States;
- a white board with dry erase markers;
- paper supplies such as poster board in several colors, butcher paper, and art notebooks;
- art and craft supplies such as glitter, a variety of paints and brushes, stamps and ink, foam shapes, stickers, feathers, pom-poms, and whatever else strikes your child's fancy;
- science experiment books and supplies such as rubber bands, balloons, baking soda, vinegar, popsicle sticks, and much more. I find myself saving extra supplies from school experiments in a science supply box so the most common items are available when needed;
- a magnifying glass and microscope;
- a nature bag with blank notebooks, colored pencils, and available field guides;
- a device to play audiobooks and music;
- games of all sorts for all subjects (We have an entire closet full of games that I've purchased very inexpensively at yard sales, curriculum sales and thrift stores.); and
- shelves and shelves of wonderful fiction, nonfiction, and reference books.

How Do I Answer People Who Don't Agree with Our Decision to Homeschool?

Homeschooling without support can be very disheartening and might even make you feel inadequate. Don't let naysayers bring you down, but prove them wrong instead. Think back to all the reasons you decided to homeschool in the first place. Take heart in the truth that your child will not be an academic or social misfit with your loving and thoughtful preparation. Pay attention to the huge rewards that shine through in your child. The naysayers will eventually begin to see the positive changes, too, and often become some of your biggest cheerleaders in the end.

Invite naysayers to watch your child perform in a production or competition. Invite them to come along on a homeschool group field trip. Let your child create homeschooling newsletters to send to them. Post a display board prominently in your home showcasing your child's great work. (This will benefit your child, too!) Involve the naysayers in a homeschooling project. For instance, ask your child to create a PowerPoint presentation of family history and ask his doubtful grandparents to tell stories and submit pictures for the project. The entire family can gather together to watch the presentation.

There will be people you won't be able to convince, and that's okay. As hard as it may be, simply try to ignore them and focus on the encouragement you find elsewhere. One piece of advice: Don't take your homeschooling woes to the naysayer. Find your sounding board somewhere else. Otherwise, you will live to regret it. Trust me.

How Do I Answer People Who Question Why My Kids Aren't in School?

Homeschoolers are often busy people. Whether you drive from this class to that play group or take a break in the day to buy supplies for a science experiment, non-homeschoolers will see you out and about. Sadly, many of these observers equate seeing you out in public during normal school hours as meaning you are not doing school. Although you should be diligent to not raise eyebrows by going to the grocery every morning at 11:00 in your pajamas, don't be worried when people ask inevitable questions about why your child isn't in school.

I simply tell the truth. "We are in school. We've just stopped in to purchase some vinegar for the giant volcano my son is building." Once people hear the exciting things we're doing, they usually go on to tell me how they wish they could homeschool their own children and how lucky we are.

What if We Have a Family Crisis or Something Else Unexpected Arises that Interferes with Schooling?

The answer depends on the situation. If there will only be a minor bump in the schooling schedule – someone has surgery that will delay school for 6 weeks, a broken arm will be in a cast for 3 weeks, or guests need to stay at your house for a month – simply take a school break and catch up on the missed days later.

If there is a more major bump – someone in the family develops a life-changing illness, the homeschooling parent must go back to work, you lose your home – homeschooling might be harder to work through, but can be done. Homeschooling parents who have had serious crises have almost always shared with me in the aftermath that school might not have been ideal, but they wouldn't have traded a day of it in order to send their children (back) to school. In fact, most of them thought they were failures as they did less structured schoolwork during the crisis, but afterward saw their children had grown by leaps and bounds both academically and emotionally. They also share that working through the crisis together made their families stronger and closer.

Sometimes, you might find it necessary to consider school again. If so, don't fret over your decision. Whether it turns out to be temporary or permanent, know you will never regret the time you were able to teach your child at home.

I hope these answers (and the rest of the book) serve to encourage you. Homeschooling in general takes dedication, patience, organization, and discipline, while homeschooling gifted children takes just a pinch more of each. I will never pretend that homeschooling is easy, but I will guarantee you rewards beyond measure!

Thank You!

I am so incredibly thankful that you chose to read this book to the end.
I pray your homeschool will be blessed beyond measure with
love, joy, creativity, and kids who love to learn!

Resources

General Resources

Throughout the book, there are specific references to many helpful resources on various topics. Below are some additional general resources that you will find helpful as you homeschool or consider homeschooling your gifted child.

Albert, D. (1999). *And the skylark sings with me: Adventures in homeschooling and community-based education.* Monroe, ME: Common Courage Press.

Albert, D. (2005). *Have fun. Learn stuff. Grow.: Homeschooling and the curriculum of love.* Monroe, ME: Common Courage Press.

Cross, T. (2005). *On the social and emotional lives of gifted kids: Understanding and guiding their development.* Waco, TX: Prufrock Press.

Delisle, J. (2006). *Parenting gifted kids: Tips for raising happy and successful children.* Waco, TX: Prufrock Press.

Delisle, J. & Galbraith, J. (2002). *When gifted kids don't have all the answers: How to meet their social and emotional needs.* Minneapolis, MN: Free Spirit.

Fertig, C. (2008). *Raising a gifted child: A parenting success handbook.* Waco, TX: Prufrock Press.

Gatto, J.T. (2002). *A different kind of teacher: Solving the crisis of American schooling*. Berkeley, CA: Berkeley Hills Books.

Gatto, J. T. & Moore, T. (2002). *Dumbing us down: The hidden curriculum of compulsory schooling*. Gabriola Island, BC: New Society.

Renzulli, J. & Reis, S. (2009). *Light up your mind: Finding a unique pathway to happiness and success*. New York, NY: Little, Brown and Company.

Rivero, L. (2008). *The homeschooling option: How to decide when it's right for your family*. New York, NY: Palgrave Macmillan.

Chapter By Chapter Resources

Chapter 2

Traditional Method of Homeschooling

All of the websites below offer curriculum packages for preschool through high school.

- A Beka – http://www.abeka.com
- Accelerated Christian Education – https://www.aceministries.com
- Alpha Omega – https://www.aop.com
- Bob Jones University Press – http://www.bjupress.com/page/Home
- Calvert School – https://www.calvertschoolmd.org/page
- Core Curriculum – http://core-curriculum.com
- K-12 – http://www.k12.com
- Moving Beyond the Page – http://www.movingbeyondthepage.com

- Oak Meadow – http://oakmeadow.com
- Rod and Staff – https://www.milestonebooks.com

Unit Study Method of Homeschooling

- A Journey Through Learning – http://www.ajourneythroughlearning.net
  This website offers lapbooking choices, which are unit studies in which small booklets are completed and glued in file folders to make a complete final project of your studies. Lapbooks are available for all grade levels.

- Beautiful Feet Books – http://bfbooks.com
  This website offers history and geography themed studies using literature as the main text. Studies can be found for elementary through high school.

- Five in a Row – http://fiveinarow.com
  Five in a Row offers guides to create small and large unit studies based on literature for the preschool through elementary child.

- Hands of a Child – http://www.handsofachild.com
  As with A Journey Through Learning, mentioned above, this website offers lapbooking choices for all ages.

- Heart of Wisdom – http://heartofwisdom.com/blog/heart-of-wisdom-shop
  This website contains Biblically-based, in-depth unit studies for all ages.

- KONOS – https://konos.com/?v=47e5dceea252
  KONOS unit studies span the course of one or more years and focus academic learning around various character qualities. The studies can be adapted for all ages.

- Moving Beyond the Page – http://www.movingbeyondthepage.com

This website sells unit studies for various ages and academic subjects. They gear their material toward gifted learners.

- NaturExplorers – https://ourjourneywestward.com
  NaturExplorers are science-based studies that focus on various nature study topics and include creative learning ideas for all ages.

- Sonlight – https://www.sonlight.com
  Sonlight offers a literature-based approach to various learning topics for all ages.

- Tapestry of Grace – http://www.tapestryofgrace.com/index.php
  This website offers Christian-based unit studies with the history of the world being the main thread through all grade levels.

Classical Method of Homeschooling

Bauer, S. W. & Wise, J. (2009). *The well-trained mind* (3rd ed.). New York, NY: W. W. Norton and Company.

Bluedorn, H. & Bluedorn, L. (2001). *Teaching the trivium*. New Boston, IL: Trivium Pursuit.

- Classical Conversations – https://www.classicalconversations.com
  This website will lead you to a list of weekly classes that might be offered in your area where your child can get a classical education via teachers who send assignments home to be completed through the week.

- Classical Homeschooling – http://www.classical-homeschooling.org/curriculum.html
  This website will educate you about classical homeschooling and offer curriculum choices for all ages.

- Covenant Home – http://www.covenanthome.com/Homeschool-Curriculum.htm
  On this website you will find curriculum choices and packages for a classical style homeschool.

- Easy Classical – http://easyclassical.com
  Here, too, you will find curriculum choices and packages for a classical style homeschool.

- Memoria Press – https://www.memoriapress.com
  Memoria Press offers various curricula for language study, literature study and other classical subjects.

- Tapestry of Grace – http://www.tapestryofgrace.com/index.php
  Although mentioned in the unit study section already, Tapestry of Grace has written their curriculum with a flair for classical education, too.

- Veritas Press – https://www.veritaspress.com
  This website offers a wide variety of classical style curriculum choices in every subject for preschool through high school.

Charlotte Mason Style of Homeschooling

Andreola, K. (1998). *A charlotte mason companion.* Quarryville, PA: Charlotte Mason Research and Supply Company.

Levison, C. (1999). *A charlotte mason education.* Toronto, Canada: Champion Press.

Macaulay, S. S. (2009). *For the children's sake.* Wheaton, IL: Crossway Books.

Mason, C. (1993). *The original homeschooling series.* Quarryville, PA: Charlotte Mason Research and Supply Company.

- Ambleside Online – http://amblesideonline.org
  This website offers free curriculum plans for all grade levels. You will need to purchase the books and texts elsewhere.

- Homeschool Highlights – http://homeschoolhighlights.com
  This website contains Charlotte Mason style curriculum choices for grammar and writing.

- Living Books Curriculum – http://charlottemasonhomeschooling.com
  As the name suggests, this website offers a curriculum fueled by literature. Christian in nature, the products are available for kindergarten through eighth grade.

- Our Journey Westward – https://ourjourneywestward.com
  This website sells the NaturExplorers science series and other creative Charlotte Mason curriculum for many subjects and grade levels.

- Queen Homeschool – http://queenhomeschool.com
  Queen Homeschool sells various Charlotte Mason style curriculum choices for many subjects and grade levels.

- Winter Promise – https://winterpromise.com
  This website offers grade leveled curriculum packages with a Charlotte Mason flair.

The Principle Approach to Homeschooling

Rose, J. B. (2002). *A guide to American Christian education for the home and school: The principle approach.* Providence, RI: Providence Foundation.

Slater, R. (1984). *Teaching & learning America's Christian history: The principle approach.* Chesapeake, VA: Foundation for American Christian Education.

- The Noah Plan – http://www.face.net

Here is only place I'm aware of for purchasing curriculum geared toward the principle approach.

Montessori Method of Homeschooling

Hainstock, E. (1997). *Teaching Montessori in the home: The pre-school years.* New York, NY: Plume.

Hainstock, E. (1997). *Teaching Montessori in the home: The school years.* New York, NY: Plume.

- Montessori Environments – http://michaelolaf.com
  On this website, you will find Montessori style toys and other materials for purchase.

- Shiller Math – https://www.shillermath.com/intro.php
  This website offers math kits in the Montessori style of teaching for preschool through elementary ages.

Unschooling Method of Homeschooling

Griffith, M. & Holt, J. (1998). *The unschooling handbook: How to use the whole world as your child's classroom.* New York, NY: Three Rivers Press.

Homeschooling and Accredited Schools

Each of the websites below offer some form of accredited school with which you can become affiliated.

- Calvert School – https://www.calvertschoolmd.org/page
- Grace Academy – http://thegraceacademy.org
- Jubilee Academy – http://thejubileeacademy.org/home
- Keystone School – http://keystoneschoolonline.com

- Laurel Springs School – https://laurelsprings.com

Distance Learning

Each of the websites below offer distance learning opportunities specifically geared toward gifted and talented students.

- Institute for Mathematics and Computer Science – https://www.eimacs.com
- John Hopkins Center for Talented Youth – https://cty.jhu.edu
- Northwestern University's Center for Talent and Development – https://www.ctd.northwestern.edu

Legal Information About Homeschooling

- Homeschool Legal Defense Association – https://hslda.org
  On this website you will find a plethora of information about the legalities of homeschooling, support groups, and other homeschooling topics.

Chapter 3
• • • • • • • • • •

Barnier, C. (2009). *The big what now book of learning styles*. Bingley, UK: Emerald Books.

Tobias, C. U. (1998). *The way they learn*. F: Tyndale House.

Willis, M. & Hodson, V. K. (1999). *Discover your child's learning style*. New York, NY: Crown.

Chapter 4

Reading

Gagen, M. (2004). *Right track reading.* Livingston, MT: Right Track Reading.

Halsted, J. W. (2002). *Some of my best friends are books: Guiding gifted readers from preschool to high school* (2nd ed.). Scottsdale, AZ: Great Potential Press.

VanTassel-Baska, J. & Stambaugh, T, (2011). *Jacob's ladder reading comprehension program, levels 1, 2, 3 & 4.* Waco, TX. Prufrock Press.

- DianneCraft.org – http://www.diannecraft.org
  On this website, Dianne Craft offers many articles and suggestions for children who struggle in various academic areas. You can also purchase materials to help your child overcome certain difficulties such as dysgraphia and dyslexia.

- Enchanted Learning Story Maps – http://www.enchantedlearning.com/graphicorganizers/storymap
  This page of Enchanted Learning offers several free story maps to print and use for reading comprehension.

- Sonlight – https://www.sonlight.com
  Sonlight is a literature-rich curriculum for all ages.

- Project Gutenberg – http://www.gutenberg.org/wiki/Main_Page
  This site offers more than 36,000 free e-books for download.

The following websites offer book lists for gifted readers of all ages.

- Our Journey Westward Living Literature Lists – https://ourjourneywestward.com/living-literature-booklists

- 101 Out-of-this-World Books for Kids Ages 8-13 – http://www.montgomeryschoolsmd.org/uploadedFiles/schools/clementems/special/101_books.pdf
- 101 Books Recommended for College-Bound Readers – http://www.alevel-sz.com/sites/default/upload/1/files/201505/college_board_recommended_books_1431003022.pdf
- 1000 Good Book List Divided by Age Groupings – http://www.classical-homeschooling.org/celoop/1000.html
- Association for Library Service to Children List of Award Winning Books – http://www.ala.org/alsc/awardsgrants/notalists
- Literature to Supplement History – http://da1.redshift.com/~bonajo/history.htm

Writing

Andreola, K. (2006). *Story starters*. Quarryville, PA: Charlotte Mason Research and Supply Company.

Cheaney, J. (2002). *Wordsmith*. Melrose, FL: Common Sense Press

Dragon SpeakNaturally. (2010). Burlington, MA. Nuance Communications.

Kemmerer, S. (2004). *Research in increments*. Telford, PA: Schoolhouse Publishing.

Kidspiration. (2011). Beaverton, OR. Inspiration Software.

Olsen, J. (2008). *Handwriting without tears*. Cabin John, MD. Handwriting Without Tears.

Rife, D. (2002). *Research and writing: Activities that explore family history*. Dayton, OH: Teaching and Learning Company.

Schwabauer, D. (2008). *One Year Adventure Novel*. Olathe, KS: Clear Water Press.

RESOURCES

Thaxton, C. (1998). *Learn to Write the Novel Way.* Fayetteville, GA: KONOS Connections.

Thaxton, C. (2004). *Write your roots.* Fayetteville, GA: KONOS Connections.

Ward, M. L. (2004). *Writing step-by-step.* Lynnwood, WA: Builder Books

Watson, S. (2006). *Jump in.* Anderson, IN: Apologia Press

- DianneCraft.org – http://www.diannecraft.org
  On this website, Dianne Craft offers many articles and suggestions for children who struggle in various academic areas. You can also purchase materials to help your child overcome certain difficulties such as dysgraphia and dyslexia.

- The Writing Kid – http://fundsforwriters.com/writingkid.htm
  This website allows you to sign up for an e-newsletter that informs you of small and large writing competitions around the country.

- The National Novel Writing Month – https://ywp.nanowrimo.org
  This site hosts a yearly writing challenge every November where participants try to write a complete novel in one month's time.

- Stapleless Book – http://www.readwritethink.org/files/resources/interactives/stapleless/index.html
  On this website you will find a free interactive story writing program from which your child can write and print a complete book.

Below are places which regularly publish writing from children.

- Bookworm: A Magazine for and by Kids – http://fobl.org.au/membership/bookworm-magazine
- Merlyn's Pen: Fiction, Essays and Poems by America's Teens – http://www.merlynspen.org
- Skipping Stones Multicultural Magazine – http://www.skippingstones.org/submissions.htm

- Stone Soup: The Magazine by Kids – https://stonesoup.com/how-to-submit-writing-and-art-to-stone-soup
- Teen Ink Magazine – http://www.teenink.com/submit
- The Write Kids Online Magazine – http://writekids.tripod.com

The following websites include information about two popular writing competitions for children and teens.

- National History Day Writing Contest – https://www.nhd.org
- Scholastic Art and Writing Competitions -http://www.artandwriting.org

Each of the websites below offer free graphic organizers for writing.

- Ed Helper – https://www.edhelper.com/teachers/graphic_organizers.htm
- Education Place – http://www.eduplace.com/kids/hme/k_5/graphorg
- Enchanted Learning – http://www.enchantedlearning.com/graphicorganizers

Grammar

Finley, R. & Karl, E. (1996). *Analytical grammar*. Raleigh, NC: Analytical Grammar.

This website offers free grammar review lessons to print for all age levels.

- Daily Grammar Archive Lessons – http://dailygrammar.com/archive.html

Spelling/Vocabulary

Adams-Gordon, B. (2006). *Spelling power* (4th ed.). Pomeroy, WA: Castlemoyle Books.

RESOURCES

Hodkinson, K. & Adams, S. (2007). *Wordly Wise.* Cambridge, MA: Educator's Publishing Service.

Kemmerer, S. (2005). Apples. Telford, PA: Schoolhouse.

Kemmerer, S. (2006). Apples 2. Telford, PA: Schoolhouse.

McCabe, D. (2008). *Sequential Spelling.* Birch Run, MI: AVKO Educational Research Foundation.

Ripple, M. (2008). *All about spelling.* Eagle River, WA: All About Learning Press.

This website offers information about how to enter the Scripps National Spelling Bee.

- Scripps National Spelling Bee – http://spellingbee.com

The following websites will lead you to various foreign language curriculum choices.

- Classical Academic Press – https://classicalacademicpress.com
- Greek-N-Stuff – http://www.greeknstuff.com
- Learnables – http://www.learnables.com
- Lively Latin – https://www.livelylatin.com
- Memoria Press – https://www.memoriapress.com
- Minimus – http://www.minimus-etc.co.uk
- Rosetta Stone – https://www.rosettastone.com

By visiting the following websites, you will find the publishers of games which are appropriate for grammar spelling and vocabulary building.

- Apples to Apples – http://www.mattel.com
- Bananagrams – http://www.bananagrams.com
- Bookworm – http://www.popcap.com
- Chunks – http://www.didax.com
- Cooking up Sentences – http://www.learningresources.com

- DICEcapades Word Pirates – http://www.haywiregroup.com
- Go to Press – http://www.learningresources.com
- Sentence Cube – http://www.dominoes.com
- Sentence Says Game – http://www.dominoes.com
- Smart Mouth Game – http://www.thinkfun.com
- Spelling Beez – http://talicor.com
- Up for Grabs – http://www.mindware.com
- You've Been Sentenced! – http://www.mcneilldesigns.com

Math/Logic

Cotter, J. (2007). *Rightstart math*. Hazelton, ND: Activities for Learning.

Demme, S. (2004). *Math-u-see*. Lancaster, PA: Math-U-See.

Rasmussen, L., Hightower, R., & Rasmussen, P. (1985). *Miquon Math*. Emoryville, CA: Key Curriculum Press.

Thompson, V., Stenmark, J. K., Cossey, R & Hill, M. (1986). *Family math*. Berkeley, CA: Lawrence Hall of Science.

West, C. (2011). *Loving living math*. Paris, KY: Our Journey Westward.

These websites offer a wide variety of critical thinking and logic curricula for all age levels.

- Critical Thinking Press – https://www.criticalthinking.com
- Prufrock Press – https://www.prufrock.com

Science

West, C. & Leach, M. (2010). *Naturexplorers*. Paris, KY: Our Journey Westward.

The following websites offer information about national level science fair competitions.

- Broadcom Masters Competition – https://student.societyforscience.org/broadcom-masters
- Intel International Science and Engineering Fair – https://student.societyforscience.org/intel-isef
- Junior Science and Humanities Symposium – https://www.jshs.org
- U.S. National BioGENEius Challenge – http://www.biotechinstitute.org/go.cfm?do=page.view&pid=2

History

Bauer, S. W. (2006). *Story of the world* (3rd ed.). Charles City, VA: Peace Hill Press.

Hobar, L. L. (2007). *Mystery of history*. Cheswold, DE: Bright Ideas Press.

This website offers literature-based history studies for elementary through high school.

- Beautiful Feet Books – http://bfbooks.com

The following websites include information about various national history and geography competitions.

- The National History Bee – https://www.aceqb.com/historybee
- National History Day Contest – https://www.nhd.org
- National Geographic Bee – https://www.nationalgeographic.org/bee

Fine Arts

This website allows children to submit photos of artwork to become part of an online gallery.

- Artsonia – https://www.artsonia.com

Philosophy, Speech and Debate

Cote, R. & Blauvelt, D. (2011). *What's your opinion?: An interactive discovery-based language arts unit for high ability learners.* Waco, TX: Prufrock Press.

Forster, P. (2005). *For instruction in righteousness: A topical reference guide for Biblical training.* Gaston, OR: Doorposts.

Jeub, C. (2001). *Jeub's complete guide to speech and debate.* Monument, CO: Training Minds.

Kaye, S. & Thomson, P. (2006). *Philosophy for teens: Examining life's big ideas.* Waco, TX: Prufrock Press.

Law, S. (2009). *Really, really big questions: About life, the universe and everything.* London, England: Kingfisher.

Porter, C. & Girsch. (2011). *Make up your mind: A classroom guide to 10 age-old debates.* Waco, TX: Prufrock Press.

Thomson, P. & Kaye, S. (2007). *More philosophy for teens: Examining reality and knowledge.* Waco, TX: Prufrock Press.

White, D. (2005). *Philosophy for kids: 40 fun questions that help you wonder about everything!* Waco, TX: Prufrock Press.

White, D. (2005). *The examined life: Advanced philosophy for kids.* Waco, TX: Prufrock Press.

This website supplies lists of children's books appropriate for pondering various philosophical issues. For each book, it gives you a summary and appropriate questions you might discuss with your child.

- Teaching Children Philosophy
  https://www.teachingchildrenphilosophy.org/BookModule/BookModule

The websites below supply information about national speech and debate competitions.

- National Christian Forensic and Communications Association – http://www.ncfca.org
- The Institute for Cultural Communicators – https://iccinc.org
- The National Forensic League – https://www.speechanddebate.org
- Toastmasters International – https://www.toastmasters.org

Leadership

This website offers information about national and state opportunities for teens to attend political leadership meetings.

- TeenPact – http://teenpact.com

The two websites below lead you to popular, nation-wide civic organizations which homeschoolers might consider joining.

- Civitan – http://www.civitan.org
- Kiwanis – http://www.kiwanis.org

Logic

Allen, M. (1987). *Primarily bears.* Fresno, CA: AIMS Education Foundation.

Bamberger, H. (1999). *Logic posters, problems and puzzles.* New York, NY: Scholastic.

Bluedorn, H. & Bluedorn, N. (2009). *The fallacy detective: 38 lessons on how to recognize bad reasoning.* Muskatine, IA: Christian Logic.

Bluedorn, H. & Bluedorn, N. (2005). *The thinking toolbox: 35 lessons that will build your reasoning skills.* Muskatine, IA: Christian Logic.

Buxton, M. L. (2007). *Math logic mysteries.* Waco, TX: Prufrock Press.

Buxton, M. L. (2008). *More math logic mysteries.* Waco, TX: Prufrock Press.

Buxton, M. L. (2011). *Math bafflers (Book 1).* Waco, TX: Prufrock Press.

Buxton, M. L. (2011). *Math bafflers (Book 2).* Waco, TX: Prufrock Press.

Carr, M. A. (2005). *More one-hour mysteries.* Waco, TX: Prufrock Press.

Carr, M. A. (2005). *One-hour mysteries.* Waco, TX: Prufrock Press.

Carr, M. A. (2010). *The great chocolate caper.* Waco, TX: Prufrock Press.

Cothran, M. (2004). *Material logic.* Louisville, KY: Memoria Press.

Cothran, M. (2000). *Traditional logic.* Louisville, KY: Memoria Press.

Critical Thinking Press. (various dates). *Mind benders.* Seaside, CA: Critical Thinking Press.

Larson, A. & Hodge, J. (2003). *Art of the argument: An introduction to the informal fallacies.* Camp Hill, PA: Classical Academic Press.

Larson, A., Hodge, J. & Johnson, S. (2010). *The discovery of deduction: An introduction to formal logic.* Camp Hill, PA: Classical Academic Press.

Risby, B. (2005). *Logic countdown.* Waco, TX: Prufrock Press.

Risby, B. (2005). *Logic liftoff.* Waco, TX: Prufrock Press

Risby, B. (2005). *Logic safari.* Waco, TX: Prufrock Press.

Risby, B. & Risby, R. (2005). *Lollipop logic.* Waco, TX: Prufrock Press.

Risby, B. & Risby, R. (2011). *Lollipop logic 2.* Waco, TX: Prufrock Press.

RESOURCES

The following websites lead you to the publisher of each of the following logic games.

- 10 days in …games – http://www.otb-games.com
- Animalogic – http://www.fatbraintoys.com
- Battleship – http://www.hasbro.com
- Blokus – http://www.mattel.com
- Checkers – any publisher
- Chess – any publisher
- Clue – http://www.hasbro.com
- Connect Four – http://www.hasbro.com
- Guess Who? – http://www.hasbro.com
- Knot So Fast – http://www.thinkfun.com
- Logic Links – http://www.mindware.com
- Mancala – any publisher
- Mastermind – http://catalog.pressmantoy.com
- MetaForms – http://www.foxmind.com
- Noodlers – http://www.mindware.com
- Qwirkle – http://www.mindware.com
- Risk – http://www.hasbro.com
- River Crossing – http://www.thinkfun.com
- Rush Hour – http://www.thinkfun.com
- Sequence – http://www.jaxgames.com
- SET – http://www.setgame.com
- Zoologic – http://www.foxmind.com

Chapter 5

Computer Curricula

- Computer Science for Kids – https://www.computerscienceforkids.com

Computer Science for Kids sells secular and Christian-based manuals for learning Microsoft computer programming languages.
- Homeschool Programming – http://www.compuscholar.com
This website sells computer programming curriculum for kids and teens.
- Mother Board Books – http://motherboardbooks.com
Mother Board Books' curriculum begins with basic computer skills and works its way through computer programming.

Integrating Technology

Mavis Beacon Teaches Typing. (2011). Los Angeles, CA: Encore Software.

Selfridge, B., Selfridge, P. & Osburn, J. (2008). *A teen's guide to creating web pages and blogs.* Waco, TX: Prufrock Press.

Stepien, W. J. (2008). *Problem-based learning with the Internet.* Waco, TX: Prufrock Press.

Typing Instructor. (2010). Pleasanton, CA: Individual Software.

Stepien, W. J., Senn, P. & Stepien, W. C. (2008). *The internet and problem-based learning: Developing solutions through the web.* Waco, TX: Prufrock Press.

Word 2010. (2010). Redmond, WA: Microsoft.

You will find a free typing lessons at these websites.

- Dance Mat Typing – http://www.kidztype.com
- TypeDojo – http://nimblefingers.com

The website below offers child-friendly information about the parts and functions of computers.

- Click-N-Learn: What's Inside a Computer – http://www.kids-online.net/learn/c_n_l.html

Online Technology Options

- Blurb – http://www.blurb.com
  On this website, you will be able to design and publish books for a fee.
- Geocaching.com – https://www.geocaching.com/play
  On this site, you can find descriptions and directions for geocaching.

Computer-based Curriculum

Switched on Schoolhouse. (2010). Rock Rapids, IA: Alpha Omega Publishing.

- Time4Learning – https://www.time4learning.com
  This website offers online curriculum in the subjects of math, language arts, science and social studies for preschool through middle school.

The following university websites offer distance learning courses online specifically for gifted and talented students.

- John Hopkins Center for Talented Youth – http://cty.jhu.edu
- Northwestern's Center for Talent Development – https://www.ctd.northwestern.edu

Safety

- Covenant Eyes – http://www.covenanteyes.com
  This website offers a family-friendly internet searching capability.

- CyberSlueth-Kids – http://cybersleuth-kids.com
  This website is a child-friendly, safe internet search engine.

Chapter 6
•••••••••

Differentiation

Adams, C., & Pierce, R. (2010). *Differentiation that really works: Strategies from real teachers for real classrooms, grades K-2 & 3-5.* Waco, TX. Prufrock Press.

Carr, M. A. (2009). *Differentiation made simple: Timesaving tools for teachers.* Waco, TX. Prufrock Press.

Drapeau, P. (2004). *Differentiated instruction: Making it work: A practical guide to planning, managing, and implementing differentiated instruction to meet the needs of all learners.* New York, NY. Scholastic.

Westphal, L. (varies). *Differentiating instruction with menus: Language arts.* Waco, TX: Prufrock Press. (Multiple levels available.)

Westphal, L. (varies). *Differentiating instruction with menus: Math.* Waco, TX: Prufrock Press. (Multiple levels available.)

Westphal, L. (varies). *Differentiating instruction with menus: Science.* Waco, TX: Prufrock Press. (Multiple levels available.)

Westphal, L. (varies). *Differentiating instruction with menus: Social studies.* Waco, TX: Prufrock Press. (Multiple levels available.)

Westphal, L. (2011). *Ready-to-use differentiation strategies.* Waco, TX. Prufrock Press. (Multiple levels available.)

Project-Based Learning

Karnes, F. A., & Stephens, K. R. (2009). *The ultimate guide to student product development and evaluation* (2nd ed.). Waco, TX: Prufrock Press.

Chapter 8

Gathercole, R. (2007). *The well-adjusted child: The social benefits of homeschooling.* Silverton, ID: Mapletree.

Klicka, C. (2007). *Socialization: Homeschoolers are in the real world.* Retrieved April 1, 2011 from HSLDA data base, http://www.hslda.org/docs/nche/000000/00000068.asp#1

Chapter 9

Bell, D. (2010). *The ultimate guide to homeschooling teens.* Anderson, IN: Apologia Press.

Berger, S. (2006). *College planning for gifted students: Choosing and getting into the right college* (3rd ed.). Waco, TX: Prufrock Press.

Berger, S. (2007). *The ultimate guide to summer opportunities for teens.* Waco, TX: Prufrock Press.

Binz, L. (2010). *Setting the records straight: How to craft homeschool transcripts and course descriptions for college admissions and scholarship.* Charleston, SC: CreateSpace.

Boles, B. (2009). *College without high school: A teenager's guide to skipping high school and going to college.* Gabriola Island, BC: New Society.

Byers, D. & Byers, C. (2008). *College-prep homeschooling: Your complete guide to homeschooling through high school.* Silverton, ID: Mapletree.

Campbell, J. (2007). *Transcripts made easy* (3rd ed.). Ashland, VA: Everyday Education.

Cohen, C. (2011). *Homeschoolers' college admissions handbook: Preparing your 12-18-year-old for a smooth transition.* New York, NY: Crown.

Cohen, C. (2010). *Homeschooling: The teen years.* New York, NY: Three Rivers Press.

Karnes, F. & Riley, T. (2005). *Competitions for talented kids: Win scholarships, big prize money, and recognition.* Waco, TX: Prufrock Press.

Hewitt, D. & Hewitt, R. (2009). *Free college resource book.* Waco, TX: Prufrock Press.

Hewitt, D. & Hewitt, R. (2010). *Get into college in 3 months or less.* Waco, TX: Prufrock Press.

Shelton, B. (1999). *Senior high: A home designed form+u+la* (3rd ed.). Longview, WA: Homeschool Seminars and Publications.

On this webpage, you will find links and information about entering college early. Browse the website for many, many more gifted topics.

- Hogie's Gifted Early College page – http://www.hoagiesgifted.org/early_college.htm

This website offers free lectures from MIT. It is one of many colleges who offer free online lectures.

- MIT – http://ocw.mit.edu/index.htm

This web group is a chat room of sorts where member discuss gifted education in general.

- TAGMAX – http://listserv.icors.org/scripts/wa-ICORS.exe?A0=TAGMAX

Chapter 10

Downes, C. (2005). *The Checklist.* Broken Arrow, OK: Author.

Hirsh, E. D. (varies). *What your __ grader needs to know.* New York, NY: Dell.

References

Bauer, S. W., & Wise, J. (2016). *The well-trained mind: A guide to classical education at home* (4th ed.). New York, NY: Norton.

Bossé. M., & Rotigel, J. (2006). *Encouraging your child's math talent: The involved parent's guide.* Waco, TX: Prufrock Press.

Brandwein, P. (1995). *Science talents in the young expressed within ecologies of achievement.* Storrs: University of Connecticut, The National Research Center on the Gifted and Talented

John Burroughs Quote, (n.d.). Retrieved from http://www.great-quotes.com/quote/254612

Campbell, A. (2007, Spring). Why study Latin and Greek? The practical, cultural and formative reason to study Classical language. *Classical Teacher Magazine.* Retrieved from http://www.memoriapress.com/articles/why-Latin-Greek.html

Classical Homeschooling. (n.d.). *What is classical education?* Retrieved from http://www.classical-homeschooling.org/introduction.html

ERIC Clearinghouse on Handicapped and Gifted Children. (1990). *Giftedness and the gifted: What's it all about?* (ERIC ED Digest #E476). Reston, VA: Author. Retrieved from http://www.nagc.org/index.aspx?id=121

Fonseca, C. (2011). *Emotional intensity in gifted students: Helping kids cope with explosive feelings.* Waco, TX: Prufrock Press.

The Foundation for American Christian Education. (n.d.). *The principle approach*. Retrieved February 4, 2011 from http://www.principleapproach.org/?page=principle_approach

Galbraith, J. (2009). *The gifted kids' survival guide* (3rd ed.). Minneapolis, MN: Free Spirit Publishing.

Gardner, H. (2004). *A multiplicity of intelligences: In tribute to Professor Luigi Vignolo*. Retrieved from http://www.howardgardner.com/papers/documents/T-100%20A%20Multiplicity%20revised.pdf

Gardner, H. (2005). *Multiple lenses on the mind*. Retrieved from http://www.howardgardner.com/docs/multiple_lenses_0505.pdf

Haroutounian, J. (1995). Talent identification and development in the arts: An artistic/educational dialogue. *Roeper Review*, 18, 112-125

Homeschool.com. (n.d.). *Frequently asked questions about Christian homeschooling with Ella Ward Gardner*. Retrieved from http://www.homeschool.com/advisors/gardener/default.asp

Infed. (2008). *Howard Gardener, multiple intelligences and education*. Retrieved from http://www.infed.org/thinkers/gardner.htm

International Montessori Index. (n.d.). *Montessori*. Retrieved from www.montessori.edu

Johnsen, S. (Ed.). (2003). *Identifying gifted students: A practical guide*. Waco, TX: Prufrock Press.

Klicka, C. (2007). *Socialization: Homeschoolers are in the real world*. Retrieved from http://www.hslda.org/docs/nche/000000/00000068.asp#1

Levande, D. (1999). Gifted readers and reading instruction. CAG *Communicator*, 30, 19-20, 41-42

REFERENCES

Montessori Mom. (n.d.). *What is the Montessori Method?* Retrieved from http://www.montessorimom.com/what-montessori-method

National Association for Gifted Children. (n.d.). *What is giftedness?* Retrieved from http://www.nagc.org/index.aspx?id=574

Peterson, N. L. (2006). *Encouraging your child's writing talent: The involved parent's guide.* Waco, TX: Prufrock Press.

Robinson, A., Shore, B. M., & Enersen, D. L. (2007). *Best practices in gifted education: An evidence-based guide.* Waco, TX: Prufrock Press.

Unschooling.com. (n.d.). FAQ's. Retrieved from http://www.unschooling.com/library/faq/index.shtml

West, C. (2009). *Living literature grammar and language arts packets.* Paris, KY: Our Journey Westward.

About the Author

Cindy is a veteran homeschooling mom of three who is blessed to live on a cattle farm in beautiful Central Kentucky. She and her husband, Steve, have loved every minute of homeschooling their bright and active children.

Cindy holds a bachelor's degree in elementary education from Eastern Kentucky University and a master's degree in education from Georgetown College. Before homeschooling, she taught kindergarten through fourth grade classrooms in the public school system.

She loves inspiring parents to teach creatively and writes practically about how to do that successfully on her blog, Our Journey Westward. Cindy also speaks regularly to homeschooling groups all over the country—and even around the world during online events.

Besides writing 25+ books of nature-based science curriculum, she has written several other popular books including *Charlotte Mason Homeschooling in 18 Easy Lessons*, *Loving Living Math*, and *Living Literature Grammar Packs*.

Your 1st – 8th graders will love the NaturExplorers studies. They all contain oodles of creative nature walks, hands-on activities, engaging research projects, printable notebooking pages, literature lists, and fun extras!

<table>
<tr><td>Animal Signs</td><td>Fruits and Nuts</td></tr>
<tr><td>Beautiful Birds</td><td>A Fungus Among Us</td></tr>
<tr><td>Butterflies Fluttery By</td><td>Hard as a Rock</td></tr>
<tr><td>Captivating Clouds</td><td>Incredible Creeks</td></tr>
<tr><td>Constant Conifers</td><td>Peaceful Ponds</td></tr>
<tr><td>Coping with the Cold</td><td>Remarkable Rain</td></tr>
<tr><td>Delgihtful Deciduous Trees</td><td>Snow and Ice</td></tr>
<tr><td>Ever-changing Erosion</td><td>Spectacular Spiders</td></tr>
<tr><td>Flying Creatures of the Night</td><td>Wonderful Wildflowers</td></tr>
<tr><td>Frogs and Toads</td><td></td></tr>
</table>

Take a look at other creative offerings at Our Journey Westward, too!

<table>
<tr><td>Charlotte Mason Homeschooling in 18 Easy Step-by-Step Lessons</td><td>Nature by the Season PK/K Winter</td></tr>
<tr><td>Loving Living Math</td><td>Nature by the Season PK/K Spring</td></tr>
<tr><td>Living Literature Grammar Packs</td><td>Nature Through the Holidays: Advent</td></tr>
<tr><td>Homeschooling Gifted and Advanced Learners</td><td>Nature Through the Holidays: Easter</td></tr>
<tr><td>100+ Creative Nature Walks</td><td>50 States Notebooking Pages</td></tr>
<tr><td>No Sweat Nature Study</td><td>Artists of the Renaissance Study</td></tr>
<tr><td>40 Outdoor Science Labs on the Go</td><td>...and more to come!</td></tr>
</table>

Made in the USA
San Bernardino, CA
01 September 2019